SHIPW[barcode]
DELIVERANCE

Politics, Culture and Modernity
in the works of Octavio Paz,
Gabriel García Márquez
and Mario Vargas Llosa

Todd Oakley Lutes

For Mona,
Thanks for being
such a great neighbor.
I hope you enjoy the book
as much as I enjoy having
finished it!
Todd

University Press of America,® Inc.
Lanham · New York · Oxford

Copyright © 2003 by
University Press of America,® Inc.
4720 Boston Way
Lanham, Maryland 20706
UPA Acquisitions Department (301) 459-3366

PO Box 317
Oxford
OX2 9RU, UK

ISBN 0-7618-2479-0 (paperback : alk. ppr.)

For my parents,
Karen and Oakley Lutes.
May I be as good a parent,
teacher and friend to my children
As you have been to me.

And for my daughter,
Lydia Kay Lutes,
who helps me experience again
the unwearied wonders of the world.

CONTENTS

LIST OF FIGURES

vii

LIST OF TABLES

PREFACE

Marshall Berman explains in his classic modernist text, *All That Is Solid Melts into Air*, that he "hoped to develop a series of visions and paradigms that could enable people to explore their own experience and history in greater detail and depth." He wanted "to write a book that would be open and stay open, a book in which readers would be able to write chapters of their own" (Berman: 9). To at least some extent, my project began as an attempt to do just that.

I wanted to explore Latin America's experience with modernity in something like the same way Berman explored Russia's in his chapter on the modernism of underdevelopment. One thing led to another, and, particularly after my encounter with the work of José Ortega y Gasset, I began to conceive of the project in a different way.

Ortega y Gasset presented both in his work and in his life a direct response to the problems of modernity that seemed to me at once more honest and more uplifting than other authors I had encountered. Ortega understood modernity philosophically but lived it creatively, with the "cheerful, hearty and even slightly wagish air that is peculiar to sport"

(Ortega y Gasset, 1961: 83). Also, Ortega's understanding of modernity put a perspective on the problem that challenged the "end of history" character given to modernity by most Western social philosophers. Instead of Nietzsche's almost apocalyptic vision of modernity's descent into nihilism, for example, Ortega frames the problem as simply "the task of our time." I found this vision of culture as the arena for living the challenges of modern life fascinating and uniquely appealing—not least because of the way it connects us and our time with the whole human experience. It also gave me an innovative way to follow through on my original plan to explore Latin American literature.

To give Ortega his due I would need to present a thorough understanding of modernity and the way others have approached it. The first half of this book (chapters 1-3) is my attempt to do that in a reasonably concise way. While far from perfect, I hope this section of the book at least succeeds in distinguishing Ortega's unique approach to modernity from those of others in the discourse.

The rest of the book returns to Berman's challenge to write additional chapters on our own experiences of modernity. I found Ortega's ideas to be generally reflected in much of Latin American literature, but the three authors covered here were especially appealing to me. I hope readers will find them a fascinating taste of the immense richness that the genre has to offer. If culture is the swimming stroke that keeps humanity afloat amid the torrential flood of modernity, as Ortega would have it, then the literary achievements of these authors must be among the most exciting ways to remember that the streets of modernity are our streets: that it is up to us to "keep on keeping on" and maybe even sometimes to rise above our shipwrecked condition.

Acknowledgments

It is never possible to acknowledge everyone who participates in the creation of a work like this book. In a stimulating intellectual environment ideas and inspiration come from just about everyone. My deepest thanks go to my daughter Lydia, my parents, Karen and Oakley Lutes, and my sister, Heather Clark. By putting up with my absences and helping me through the most difficult times they have perhaps sacrificed the most to see this project come to completion. Academically, my most important mentors have been Lawrence A. Scaff, Edward J. Williams, and Phillip C. Chapman. Larry Scaff inspired the project with his seminars on modernity and Max Weber. Whatever I have right about Weber I owe to him, though my errors remain my own. Ed Williams introduced me to Latin American Political Thought and to José Ortega y Gasset. He has also been an important friend and mentor through the process of getting the manuscript ready for publication. Phil Chapman helped me to pull all the disparate elements of the project together and complete it. My students are a constant source of inspiration and enthusiasm. Thanks to Cary

Nederman for his thorough reading of the manuscript and helpful suggestions. Additional thanks to Holly Shinn, who edited, proofread and otherwise polished the manuscript for publication. The cooperation and support of my colleagues here at the University of Arizona South and at the Department of Political Science at the University of Arizona, Tucson, is also appreciated. Thanks also go to the authors and publishers listed below, who graciously allowed me to quote from their material. Finally to all those who helped but are not named here, my sincere thanks.

Excerpts from EQUUS: A PLAY IN TWO ACTS by Peter Shaffer, copyright © 1973 (Samuel French, Inc.), reprinted by permission from Peter Shaffer.

From GABRIEL GARCÍA MÁRQUEZ by George R. McMurray, translated by Helen Lane, copyright © 1977 by Frederick Ungar Publishing. Reprinted by permission of The Continuum International Publishing Group.

Excerpts from GABRIEL GARCÍA MÁRQUEZ: ONE HUNDRED YEARS OF SOLITUDE by Michael Wood, copyright © 1990 by Cambridge University Press. Reprinted with the permission of Cambridge University Press.

Submitted excerpt from THE GREEN HOUSE BY MARIO VARGAS LLOSA, TRANSLATED BY GREGORY RABASSA copyright © 1968 by Harper & Row Publishers, Inc. Reprinted by permission of HarperCollins Publishers Inc.

Excerpt from ITINERARY, copyright © 1994 by Octavio Paz, English Translation copyright © 1999 by Jason Wilson, reprinted by permission of Harcourt, Inc.

Excerpts from THE LABYRINTH OF SOLITUDE AND THE OTHER MEXICO, RETURN TO THE LABYRINTH OF SOLITUDE, MEXICO AND THE UNITED STATES, THE PHILANTHROPIC OGRE by Octavio Paz, translated by Lysander Kemp, Yara Milos, and Rachel Phillips Belash, copyright © 1985 by Grove Press, Inc., reprinted by permission of Grove/Atlantic, Inc.

From LOVE IN THE TIME OF CHOLERA by Gabriel García Márquez, translated by Edith Grossman, copyright © 1988 by Alfred A. Knopf, a division of Random House, Inc. Used by permission of Alfred A. Knopf, a division of Random House, Inc.

Excerpts from MAKING WAVES by Mario Vargas Llosa, translated by John King. Translation copyright © 1996 by Farrar, Straus & Giroux, Inc., reprinted by permission of Farrar, Straus and Giroux, LLC.

From ON THE GENEALOGY OF MORALS AND ECCE HOMO by Friedrich Nietzsche, translated by Walter Kaufman, copyright © 1988 by Random House, Inc. Translated & edited, with commentary by Walter Kaufman. Used by permission of Random House, Inc.

Excerpt from ONE EARTH, FOUR OR FIVE WORLDS REFLECTIONS ON CONTEMPORARY HISTORY by Octavio Paz, English translation copyright © 1985 by Harcourt, Inc., reprinted by permission of the publisher.

The Modern Mind

> *The fate of our times is characterized by rationalization and intellectualization and, above all, by the "disenchantment of the world." Precisely the ultimate and most sublime values have retreated from public life either into the transcendental realm of mystic life or into the brotherliness of direct and personal human relations.*
>
> Max Weber (1946: 155)
> "Science as a Vocation"

The modern age at once excites and disappoints the critical mind. Now, at the dawn of the twenty-first century, humans have achieved such mastery of the world that nothing seems beyond our ultimate achievement. The world is full not of possibilities, but of perfectibilities. What can be perceived can be understood, and what can be understood can be mastered. We are measuring sublimation on Mars, creating new chemical elements, and mapping the nucleotide pairs of our own chromosomes. Even death, the universal division between gods and mortals, now seems a comprehensible daemon. Today humanity is overtaking its most far-fetched dreams of mastering nature.

Yet human world-mastery has not come without doubts and misgivings. Critics complain that the pace of modern living has taken from society something essential for human happiness. Popular culture is rife with nostalgia for the old days before the achievements of science and medicine. Personal testimonials rail against modern social problems almost at the same time that they revel in the technological wonders of the age. Clearly, the modern mind is perplexed about its possibilities.

The problems that come with modernity are familiar to all who struggle to make their day to day lives rewarding in the complex societies of the developed world. Headlines about crime, gang violence, and urban riots keep doubts about progress conspicuous and often represent only the flashy surface of deeper problems such as delinquency, broken families, ignorance, teen pregnancy, suicide, and the flight to drugs. Critics and prophets of various distinction have assured anyone who will listen that these social ills (and the many other real or imagined evils of the speaker's particular canon) should be attributed to one or several of a variety of causes. A commonly fingered villain, for example, is the weakening of the family unit as the primary cohesive force holding society together. Another is the lack of proper education and parenting for children today. More sophisticated, but along the same lines, is Alan Bloom's contention that cultural pluralism has opened up an intellectual void in America that effectively undermines any sense of social responsibility amid its assault on the concept of truth (Bloom, 1987).

A common thread runs through most of these diagnoses. One way or another, each argues that moral decline is ultimately responsible for the weakness of modern society. The dissolution of the family is a problem because it deprives youth of the experience of a supportive, loving community (and the moral knowledge such experience imparts). Bureaucratized education and poor parenting rob children of moral role models, and cultural pluralism undercuts the established value system and promotes arrogant amorality in individuals. Indeed, despite the plurality of competing diagnoses, there is substantial agreement that the basic cause of today's social problems is a crisis of morality. Though many blame the weakness of modern social institutions for this moral crisis, at least one school of social thought contends that such institutional attenuation is really only symptomatic of a much larger, underlying problem relating to the modern understanding of morality itself.

"The problem of modernity," as it has come to be known, is the focal point for an intellectual school of thought that contends the rise of science and reason in the modern age has forever changed the way morality and ethics can be construed in human society. Made up primarily of academic social theorists in Europe and America, the school argues that the cause of this change is not the weakness of modern institutions but rather the dynamic nature of human society itself. This approach needs to be taken seriously, as it presents a persuasive, coherent picture of social trends that could well have resulted in the moral crisis being experienced today.

The first three chapters of this study are devoted to exploring the concept of modernity itself. Chapter one establishes a foundational understanding of modernity based primarily on the work of German sociologist Max Weber. Chapter two focuses on the works of Friedrich Nietzsche and Max Weber to present a summary of the philosophical, cultural, and political problems that arise from the modern condition. Chapter three rounds out the discussion with a consideration of the typical "Western" responses to modernity offered by the most prominent social critics of the modern era. Chapter three also introduces an alternative "non-western" response to the problems of modernity based on the work of Spanish philosopher and social critic José Ortega y Gasset.

Chapter four makes the case that Ortega's approach to modernity is reflected clearly in much of what Marshall Berman, among others, refers to as "the literature of underdevelopment." Specifically, chapter four argues that Ortega's approach to modernity is not only reflected in the literature of underdevelopment, but that this literature is itself acting out Ortega's philosophical response to the problems of modernity. Nowhere is this "acting out" clearer than in the Spanish literature of Latin America; a tradition that builds directly upon Ortega's ideas.

The final three chapters examine some of the major works of contemporary Latin American literature in the light of both modernity theory and Ortega's response to the problems of modernity. Three of Latin America's most prominent authors are considered in these chapters: Octavio Paz of Mexico, Gabriel García Márquez of Colombia, and Mario Vargas Llosa of Peru. Chapter five contends that the way these authors portray time and reality reflects an understanding of the philosophical problem of modernity similar to the one presented more directly by José Ortega y Gasset. Chapter six takes on the cultural problem of modernity, arguing with Ortega that the struggle against the overwhelming solitude of modernity is what defines our age and showing how Paz, García Márquez, and Vargas Llosa all find the energy to carry on this struggle within their understanding of "love." Chapter seven brings the study to its conclusion by considering the political problem of modernity and how Paz, García Márquez, and Vargas Llosa find dignity in the struggle to move from a politics of power to a politics of criticism practiced within the traditions of democracy and toleration. Following Ortega y Gasset, this struggle is perhaps not so much a "solution" to the problems of modernity as it is deliverance from the worst consequence of nihilism: the despair that threatens to undermine all modern struggles before they have begun. As Paz concludes, we have not and will not solve the contradictions of modernity, but "with them and through them" we engage in the struggle that grants dignity to the human enterprise and defines the beauty of our "truly original culture" (Paz 1991: 41).

CHAPTER 1

Conceptualizing Modernity

> *The Puritan wanted to work in a vocation [wollte
> Berufsmensch sein]; we must do so. For when
> asceticism was carried out of monastic cells into
> vocational life and began to dominate
> inner-worldly morality, it helped to build the
> tremendous cosmos of the modern economic
> order. This order is now bound to the technical
> and economic presuppositions of mechanical,
> machinelike production, which today determines
> with irresistible force the lifestyle [Lebensstil] of
> all individuals born into this mechanism, not only
> those directly engaged in economic enterprise,
> and perhaps will determine it until the last ton of
> fossil coal is burned.*

> Max Weber (1946: 155)
> *The Protestant Ethic and the Spirit of Capitalism*
> (Quoted and translated in Scaff: 88)

"Modernity" is best understood as a distinctive way of living or "form"
of life; the "modern era" is the historical time period in which this
lifestyle is practiced. Most philosophers and social theorists date the
beginning of the modern era to the eighteenth century. The
Enlightenment set the tone for the new age, ushering in a style of living
based on reason and the pursuit of scientific inquiry. At the time, this

new approach to life offered a way out of the suffering and static despair of the middle ages. Now, the modern commitment to reason as a way of life patterns the existence of millions who live and work in the hyper-rational workplaces, states, and information networks of the early twenty-first century.

Modernity as a lifestyle set in motion a number of trends that have continued to shape Western societies in consistent and predictable ways since the eighteenth century. These transformational characteristics of modernity are well-known among social theorists and continue to be the dynamic agents fashioning the future of today's advanced industrial, commercial, urban, and information-intensive societies.[1] Four main trends are commonly identified: fragmentation and specialization, secularization, the separation of the spheres, and rationalization (see table 1.1).

FOUR CHARACTERISTIC TRANSFORMATIONS

Fragmentation and specialization describes a twofold process in which modern influences first break down existing social unities and then lead to a process of structural differentiation in which human activities, institutions and roles become specialized and separated from one another. Fragmentation begins with the erosion of social unities and shared understandings.

Since the Enlightenment, many of the bonds that united individuals and groups through shared experience and interdependence have dissolved under the pressures of modernity. Freud gave what is perhaps one of the most poignant testimonials to the power of modernity to break apart social unities in the midst of a discussion of modern technology:

> If there had been no railway to conquer distances, my child would never have left his native town and I should need no telephone to hear his voice; if traveling across the ocean by ship had not been introduced, my friend would not have embarked on his sea-voyage and I should not need a cable to relieve my anxiety about him. (Freud: 35)

The mobility introduced by technology has made communities less stable and social unities less certain. But technology is only one modern influence that makes the preservation of social ties more difficult. There are also such equally modern innovations as individualism, economic competition and expansion, and urbanization. All of these forces can lead to the dissolution of even once-powerful social wholes. In pre-modern times, communities tended to be relatively self-sufficient, based on extended-family households and local economies. Now...

Characteristic Transformations	Brief Definition	Explanation & Examples
Fragmentation and Specialization	1) Breakdown of existing social unities; 2) structural differentiation of human activities, institutions and roles	Increasing division of labor, interest groups, non-extended families, divorce, single-parent families, prevalence of self-interest and atomization in general
Secularization	The trend toward basing morality on philosophical foundations, and associated "waning of sacredness"	The sacred (in Durkheim's sense as symbolizing beliefs held strongly by the community) loses its meaning; "Holy Days" to holidays, etc.
Separation of the Spheres	The appearance of competing value systems associated with particular "spheres" of life activity	Separation of value-systems operative in economic, political, and cultural spheres of life (and probably others — 'familial', 'erotic', etc.)
Rationalization	The process by which instrumental-formal rationality becomes dominant in modern society	Prevalence of instrumental-rational action and formal rationality in social action; worth set by formal rather than substantive criteria

Table 1.1 Summary of the Characteristic Transformations of Modernity

> the trend is toward a more fragmented social life; isolation of
> individuals replaces the isolation of communities.   People
> participate segmentally, that is, on the basis of special interests and
> occasions rather than as whole persons, and they do so in groups
> that are themselves only weakly bound into the rest of society.
> (Selznick: 5)

Although most evident in the movement from extended families to detached nuclear families, the trend toward fragmentation is also responsible for continuing breakdown in the family unit. The increasing social tolerance (or acceptance) of divorce, delinquency and single parenting may be seen as evidence of modern influences toward atomization and separation. Of course, families continue to actively resist these trends, but where in premodern times society worked to hold families and groups together, now it is the caustic influence.

The process of specialization is similar to fragmentation except that it focuses not on the breaking apart of old unities, but on the reorganization of human activities, institutions, and roles into new patterns.   More precisely stated, occupational activities and social practices that were once fused have gone through a process of structural differentiation (specialization) that has rendered them separate and distinct from each other. Where individuals once engaged in a rounded composite of activities practiced in essentially similar ways across the entire community, people's lives are now uniquely variegated compilations of highly specialized identities. Instead of experiencing life as a whole, modern men and women experience life piecemeal, through a variety of distinct roles, arenas, and group-affiliations.

One example of this kind of modern segmentation of life is the separation of religion and community. Religious leaders generally do not participate in community affairs in their religious capacity, but rather by adopting roles more appropriate to that forum (i.e. voter, citizen). This type of separation was not characteristic of premodern times. Similar kinds of structural differentiation (or "specialization" in social roles and affiliations) have taken place in many areas of life, including the practices of production and consumption, education and parenting, family life and work, ownership and management, and private and public life (Selznick: 4).

Secularization, the second characteristic transformation of modernity, gathered strength following the Enlightenment with the increasing accomplishments of science and reason. As religious beliefs gave way to science and the pursuit of reason, people sought to justify morality and ethical behavior on the basis of secular philosophical foundations. But this turned out to be a precarious venture, as it desiccated cultural symbols and removed the moral order from the world of everyday experience by rendering it abstract, distant, and dependent on the eccentricities of individual thought. This process can be understood as a gradual "waning of sacredness" in modern societies (Selznick: 5).

According to Emile Durkheim, "the sacred" is a manifestation of the influence of the community on the individual, the guiding force of what he calls the "collective consciousness": "It is in spiritual ways that social pressure exercises itself" (Durkheim: 239). Individuals take refuge in the sacred (collectively approved and reinforced patterns of behavior) and find in the doing of one's duty "a feeling of comfort... which sustains them" (Durkheim: 242).

Over time, the sacred (as the expression of the collective consciousness) becomes 'clothed' in an object or symbol that Durkheim terms a "totem." Although this totem is no more than a representation of the solidarity of the community, the individual members of the community lose sight of this fact and transfer their respect from the community solidarity, as such, to the totem itself (Durkheim: 252).[2] The object or symbol becomes sacred in the sense that "it is forbidden to touch it, that is to say, to deny it or to contest it" (Durkheim: 244). This is so because to deny the thing would be to deny the community itself, which takes shape around a collective agreement about what the thing represents. Durkheim even claims that without this outer representation of the solidarity of a community, no community could possibly be formed or kept together (Durkheim: 265-266).

In modernity, it is exactly these symbols and "totems" that become threatened by secularization. The process unfolds in the following way. In the pre-modern world, following Durkheim, the world is divided between things sacred and things profane. (The profane is everything that is normal in the sense that it is not related to the collective consciousness exerted by the community.) As reason gathers strength in the Enlightenment with the coming of the modern age, science takes over many of the functions performed by religion in pre-modern times, including the responsibility for establishing the "demarcation criterion" between things sacred (scientific) and things profane. Many of the old "religious" totems are dashed to pieces at this point as science forges its own version of "the sacred":

> The prohibition of criticism is an interdiction [that] proves the presence of something sacred. Even today, howsoever great may be the liberty which we accord to others, a man who should totally deny progress or ridicule the human ideal to which modern societies are attached, would produce the effect of a sacrilege. There is at least one principle which those the most devoted to the free examination of everything tend to place above discussion and to regard as untouchable, that is to say, as sacred: this is the very principle of free examination. (Durkheim: 244)

Thus through the principle of free examination (i.e. the search for truth using the tools of observation and reason), science is able both to undermine the old religious foundations of commitment and belief and to establish its own version of the sacred. This is the first half of the secularization process.

Science's new preeminence in society was not, in itself, a problem, though eventually it did have very serious consequences. Specifically, by the early twentieth century (or the late modern age) it was clear that secular philosophy had been unsuccessful in its attempts to justify any moral or ethical code on the basis of scientific reason. As a result, science was unable to bestow the status of sacredness on any new symbol or belief system. The principle of free examination itself began to slowly erode the whole concept of any distinction between the sacred and the profane, and the result was a true "waning of sacredness" on all fronts.[3]

The secularization process in modernity is completed when "the sacred" becomes distant and—as Durkheim warned—society begins to fall apart. It is very significant (and unique in the history of ideas), that no new sources of commitment and belief are currently being created to replace those gutted by modernity.

The Separation of the Spheres is the third characteristic transformation of modernity and it is a consequence of both the trend toward fragmentation and specialization and the process of secularization. As life becomes more compartmentalized into its various aspects (the result of fragmentation and specialization), and as the old unifying beliefs and symbols lose their status as embodiments of the "collective consciousness" of the community (the result of the secularization process), the search for a new source of life-affirming value turns to the fragmented "spheres" of life experience that surface with modernity. What emerges is not only a plurality of arenas in which different kinds of life experiences take place, but a plurality of competing value systems—each valid within its own sphere, but none valid across the whole of life in any way comparable to pre-modern value systems. Thus the "separation of the spheres" is much more than a simple partitioning of life; it is, as Max Weber would explain, a division of the world between contentious gods whose "attitudes toward life are

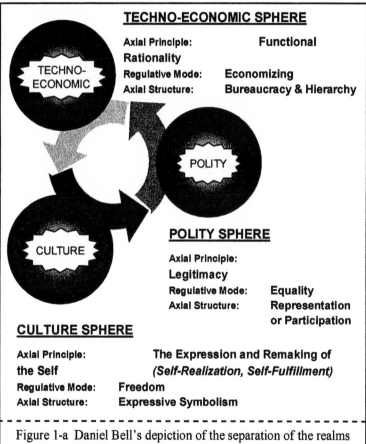

TECHNO-ECONOMIC SPHERE

Axial Principle:	**Functional**
Rationality	
Regulative Mode:	**Economizing**
Axial Structure:	**Bureaucracy & Hierarchy**

POLITY SPHERE

Axial Principle:	
Legitimacy	
Regulative Mode:	**Equality**
Axial Structure:	**Representation**
	or Participation

CULTURE SPHERE

Axial Principle:	**The Expression and Remaking of**
the Self	*(Self-Realization, Self-Fulfillment)*
Regulative Mode:	**Freedom**
Axial Structure:	**Expressive Symbolism**

Figure 1-a Daniel Bell's depiction of the separation of the realms (spheres) in modernity (Bell: 10-14).

irreconcilable" and whose "struggle can never be brought to a final conclusion" (Weber 1946: 152).

Exactly what competing value spheres emerge in modernity is a matter of debate among theorists, though nearly all agree on the presence of at least three: the economic, the political, and the aesthetic or cultural. Daniel Bell has given one of the clearest summaries of this picture of the separation of the spheres in his book *The   Cultural Contradictions of Capitalism* (see figure 1-a). His division is between the "techno-economic structure," the "polity," and "culture":

> The techno-economic order is concerned with the organization of the production and the allocation of goods and services... In modern society, the axial principle is *functional rationality*, and the regulative mode is *economizing*. Essentially, economizing means efficiency, least cost, greatest return, maximization, optimization, and similar measures of judgment about the employment and mix of resources... The axial structure is bureaucracy and hierarchy... [Bell's Italics]
>
> The polity is the arena of social justice and power... The axial principle of the polity is legitimacy, and in a democratic polity it is the principle that power can be held and governance exercised only with the consent of the governed. The implicit condition is the idea of equality... The axial structure is that of representation or participation...
>
> By culture... I mean... the realm of symbolic forms and... more narrowly the arena of expressive symbolism: those efforts... which seek to explore and express the meanings of human existence in some imaginative form... Modern culture is defined by [the] extraordinary freedom to ransack the world storehouse and to engorge any and every style it comes upon. Such freedom comes from the fact that the axial principle of modern culture is the expression and remaking of the "self" in order to achieve self-realization and self-fulfillment... It is a reaching out for all experience; nothing is forbidden... (Bell: 11-14)

Of course, there is no agreement about the exact nature of the realms competing in modernity. Max Weber, for example, identifies at least seven orders—"the familial, religious, economic, political, aesthetic, erotic, and intellectual (scientific) life-orders or spheres of life activity and value" (see figure 1-b)—and there is evidence to suggest

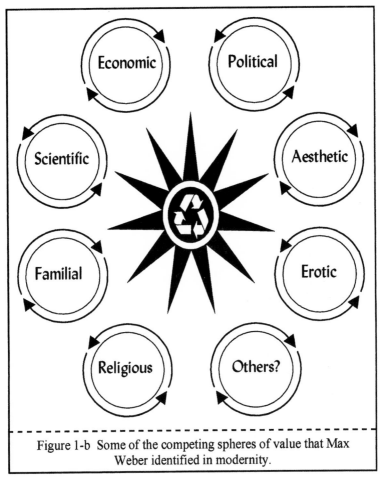

Figure 1-b Some of the competing spheres of value that Max
Weber identified in modernity.

that he thought "any number of competing orders or value-spheres at
different levels of generality may be formed out of modern experience"
(Scaff: 94, 96).

The specific depiction of the competing value spheres in modernity
is less important than the consequences of the separation itself, however,
for it is this division that both creates divided souls in modern
individuals who fail to choose only one "god" from the pantheon
(leading to anomie, alienation, etc.) and profoundly increases the
influence of economic rationality because of the chaos let loose among
and inside of the other value spheres. The economic sphere (Bell's

"techno-economic" realm) achieves a preponderance of influence because, unlike the other spheres, its content is simple, internally-consistent, and uncontested within its own realm. This content is, of course, economic or means-ends rationality in which value is counted in terms of monetary costs and benefits and profits should be maximized. It is the rise of this kind of rationality, and its consequences for modern society, that is the basis for the last characteristic transformation of modernity.

Rationalization is the final, and perhaps most sweeping characteristic transformation of modernity. At its simplest, rationalization simply "signifies an increase in rationality" (Wellmer: 40), but Enlightenment-era social thinkers quickly realized that the concept had revolutionary potential as well.

Before the Enlightenment (and for a long time thereafter), the predominant social mechanisms for organization, advancement, and control were kinship, patronage, and social status. This feudal social order remained rigid and impenetrable until the Enlightenment's emphasis on the importance of human reason introduced new economic and organizational models that made alternative lifestyles possible. Bureaucracy, for example, with its formal legal rules of procedure, made ability and knowledge the criteria for advancement and efficiency the criteria for success. Voluntary agreement, or 'contract' replaced the patrimonial standard of personal loyalty as the keystone of the system, and impersonal rule of law became the mechanism of social control. Because these new forms were able to outperform and outproduce their feudal counterparts, rationalization's first achievement became the overthrow of the feudal order.

There is much to be praised in these changes. Freedom and fairness make great strides because of rationalization, as do efficiency, excellence, professional accountability, and social tolerance. Indeed, nearly every post-Enlightenment social theorist praised the rationalization process for bringing so many good things with modernity. This popular interpretation of the rationalization process remained almost without significant opposition until early in the twentieth century.

Max Weber was the first to assert that rationalization has a greater significance for modern culture. While not dismissing the positive social achievements that resulted from the Enlightenment's emphasis on reason, Weber took a much more dismal view of the long-term effects of rationalization. Specifically, he argued that despite the early achievements of modernity, "the 'rationalization' of society does not carry any utopian perspective, but is rather likely to lead to an increasing imprisonment of modern man in dehumanized systems of a new [i.e. non-feudal] kind" (Wellmer: 41). To fully appreciate Weber's argument, it is necessary to understand his conception of rationality.

WEBER'S CONCEPTION OF "RATIONAL ACTION"

Weber says that reason is one type of "basis for certainty in understanding" among human beings and that it can be either "logical" or "mathematical" in nature (Weber 1968: 5).[4] As a "basis for certainty in understanding," reason functions as a method for achieving interpersonal agreement concerning "meaning." The way it establishes such agreement (in both its logical and mathematical forms) is by associating elements in a set of concepts or phenomena on the basis of known (or agreed) relationships. Thus reason, in plain terms, is a way to establish shared understandings about the world and the way it works through the application of logical thinking.

As Weber shows, it is the application of reason, in this sense, that makes deliberate action and planning possible in a social environment. Thus reason also forms the basis for the first two categories of Weber's typology of 'social action' (defined as socially meaningful action—see Weber 1968: 22). The two kinds of rational action-orientations are "instrumentally rational" (*zweckrational*) action and "value-rational" (*wertrational*) action (Weber 1968: 24-25).[5]

Weber defined "instrumentally rational" social action as deliberate action "determined by expectations as to the behavior of objects in the environment and of other human beings" (Weber 1968: 24). This is often referred to (even by Weber) as the 'means-ends action-orientation'. "Value-rational" social action, in contrast, is deliberate action "determined by a conscious belief in the value for its own sake of some ethical, aesthetic, religious, or other form of behavior, independently of its prospects for success" (Weber 1968: 24-25). Both of these action-orientations are "rational" in Weber's scheme because both involve deliberate, planned action related to shared meanings concerning social reality. The distinction between the two is made according to the original basis on which the action was taken: if it was taken on the basis of expectations about human behavior or events in the world, then it was instrumentally rational"; if it was taken to comply with a belief without thought of worldly consequences, it was "value-rational."

Within each of these categories of social action Weber went on to distinguish between the two types of reason identified earlier: mathematics and logic or, as Weber more often refers to them, "formal rationality" and "substantive rationality" (Weber 1968: 85-86).[6] The distinction between these two types of rationality is made on the basis of how the "certainty in understanding" that (in its infinite manifestations) determines all types of rational action is established.

'Formal rationality of action' is the extent to which an action is based on mathematical calculation or the demands of "the process" rather than ultimate ends or goals that exist outside the scope of a given system. For example, selling a treasured old clunker can often be a painful experience because the money economy values items according to their present or expected market situation and disallows any alternative forms of valuation (such as those based on sentiment or emotional attachment). Similarly, Weber points out that formal justice is meant to be a self-perpetuating system in which "legal certainty" serves both to perpetuate the system and minimize (or eliminate) appeals to ideals beyond the scope of the rule of law.

'Substantive rationality of action', in contrast, is the degree to which rational social action is "shaped... under some criterion (past, present, or potential) of ultimate values" (Weber 1968: 85). Note that "ultimate values" are here very different than the 'system goals' of formal rationality:

> The concept of "substantive rationality"... conveys only one element common to all "substantive" analyses: namely, that they do not restrict themselves to note the purely formal and (relatively) unambiguous fact that action is based on "goal-oriented" rational calculation with the technically most adequate available methods, but apply certain criteria of ultimate ends, whether they be ethical, political, utilitarian, hedonistic, feudal (*ständisch*), egalitarian, or whatever, and measure the results of the economic action, however formally "rational" in the sense of correct calculation they may be, against these scales of "value rationality" or "*substantive* goal rationality." (Weber's italics, 1968: 85-86)

The point of making these distinctions and bringing up so many technical definitions is both to show how Weber's central thesis concerning rationalization crystallized in his own thought and to clarify the persuasiveness of his argument to modern readers. To see where the argument is going, the two typologies just discussed must be crossed in a matrix. The result is a table with four cells, each representing a specific kind of rational social action (see table 1.2).

Briefly, Weber's contention is that in modernity, the logic of formal rationality and instrumentally rational (expectation-determined or means-ends) social action is strengthened dramatically by the rise of science, while the importance of value-rational action and substantive rationality fades with the progress of secularization. The transformation is general and becomes widespread over time until one kind of reason, that represented by the upper-left cell in table 1.2, comes to dominate all the others. Thus for Weber "rationalization" does not signify only "an increase in rationality" (as previous theorists had suggested), but rather the growing importance—even 'imperialism'—of one kind of rationality over all other forms.

Type of Rationality	Type of Social Action	
	Instrumental Rational Action	Value Rational Action
Formal Rationality	Action determined by expectations (about behavior and events) and conforming to a value defined in a system of formal rules.	Action determined by belief (without regard for consequences) and conforming to a value defined in a system of formal rules.
Substantive Rationality	Action determined by expectations (about behavior and events) and designed to be in accordance with some criterion of ultimate value.	Action determined by belief (without regard for consequences) and designed to be in accordance with some criterion of ultimate value.

Table 1.2 Weber's typology of rational social action crossed with his typology of rationality.

The extent to which this transformation has occurred can be illustrated by applying the typology introduced in table 1.2 to competing 'value spheres' in modernity (see the section on "the separation of the spheres," pp. 10-14). For simplicity, the following illustrations will use the three spheres delineated by Daniel Bell (1976).

Table 1.3 depicts characteristic types of action in the "techno-economic" sphere classified according to the typology introduced in table 1.2. The modern "system" that defines formal rationality in this sphere functions according to the systematic rules for calculating economic costs and benefits and is founded on the supreme value of money. The upper left hand cell (instrumental rational action involving formal rationality) is thus the cell of pure cost accounting. Its strength in modernity is easily gauged by comparing its content to that of the other cells in the matrix. Not surprisingly, these other cells seem very weak by comparison, even to the point where some of their characteristic activities are commonly thought of as "irrational."

The upper-right cell, for example, retains the value given to money by the economic system, but uses it in actions guided by beliefs rather than expectations about market consequences. The result is a class of activities in which money (or labor) is donated without any thought for the economic repercussions of the act. The thing is done simply because it is considered the right thing to do. Such actions cannot be considered completely 'rational' in a modern economic sense because they almost always result in a sub-optimal monetary condition for the actor. Tithing is one example of this kind of activity, in which ten percent of an individual's income is donated without any kind of market return (present or potential). Productive labor in a monastic order (or any similar community-based productive association) involves a similar kind of donation—this time in the form of time and labor—though here the 'irrationality' only exists to the degree that the value of the labor supersedes the value of market-estimable returns like room and board. In both of these cases, the donation of money or labor is determined by beliefs yet calculated or organized according to the imperatives of the market system. Tithing is calculated as a percentage of income, for example. Similarly, a monastic community that could not organize itself well enough to meet the market imperatives of its situation would soon dissolve. Thus these actions are determined by beliefs, but defined by systematic rules for the calculation of economic costs and benefits.

In the lower left cell of table 1.3 the parameters of the action are inverted, but the results equally irrational from the standpoint of the modern economic system. Here action is determined by expectations about the behavior of people and objects in the environment, but it is also designed to be in accordance with some criterion of ultimate value unrelated to the market system. In this cell are found, for example, activities like donating money or time to charities that seek to achieve some state of affairs consistent with an actor's beliefs about ultimate value. Action is thus taken with an eye toward consequences, but it is measured according to the ultimate value being served, not the value of money. Such actions are not rational in the modern economic sense because the results being sought are not valued in the currency of

ACTION IN THE "TECHNO-ECONOMIC" VALUE SPHERE

Type of Rationality	Type of Social Action	
	Instrumental Rational Action	Value Rational Action
Formal Rationality	Market-oriented action determined by expectations and conforming to value as defined by the systematic rules for calculation of economic costs and benefits. **For Example:** - Profit Maximizing - Cost Accounting - Bureaucratic Administration	Market-oriented action determined by belief and conforming to value as defined by the systematic rules for calculation of economic costs and benefits. **For Example:** - Tithing - Community Work Schedules (such as in a monastic order)
Substantive Rationality	Market-oriented action determined by expectations and consciously designed to be in accordance with some (non-system-based) criterion of ultimate value. **For Example:** - Willful, non tax exempt, and/or anonymous monetary or labor-based contributions to charities, churches and political causes.	Market-oriented action determined by belief (without regard for consequences) and consciously designed to be in accordance with some criterion of ultimate value. **For Example:** - Taking a vow of poverty - Gift-giving - Devoting life to service of a cause or master

Table 1.3 A Weberian typology of rational action and forms of rationality in the "techno-economic" value sphere.

'money' alone and usually end up in some kind of net monetary loss to the actor. (Note that to the extent the donation was given simply because it was "tax deductible," or similarly valuable in an economic sense, it would be more characteristic of action in the upper-left [instrumental-formal rational action] cell.) Revenge (where money is the means) is a classic negative example of this kind of action.

The final, lower-right cell is wholly irrational from the standpoint of the modern economic system because it completely disparages the value of money. Actions are here determined by beliefs and designed to be in accordance with some criterion of ultimate value other than money. Examples might include such grand actions as becoming a priest or monk, taking a vow of poverty, or devoting one's life to service of a cause or a human 'master'; or they could also include such simple acts as gift-giving. In all of these cases, the action in question is neither determined by expectations about the consequences of one's action nor valued in monetary terms.

Table 1.4 is similar to table 1.3 except that it depicts characteristic types of action in the "polity" sphere. The meaning of the different kinds of action in each cell is the same, except that here formal rational action is oriented to the values of legitimacy and equality as defined by the system of laws (see figure 1-a, on Bell's depiction of the "separation of the spheres"—p. 11) instead of to the market system of calculation. Once again, the strength of the upper left cell in relation to the others in modern times is obvious simply from the examples given.

Less obvious, but just as important is the movement that has taken place since premodern times. In both table 1.3 and table 1.4, Weber's argument is that the rationalization process makes the upper left cell dominant. Where political decisions had been made substantively on the basis of a ruler's commands, now they are made formally on the basis of law. Where economic behavior (agricultural production) was once governed by the seasons, and the pantheon of gods associated with natural phenomena, now it depends on the formal workings of the market. Figure 1-c is a graphic illustration of the general trend of this movement, although Weber almost certainly had a more specific pattern in mind when he wrote *The Protestant Ethic and the Spirit of Capitalism.* (This 'more specific pattern' will be examined in the next section.) For now, the important thing is to recognize that "instrumental formal rational action" is dominant in modernity and that this constitutes a fundamental change from pre-modern times.

Only in the sphere of culture is the dominance of the instrumental-formal cell challenged in any important way. As table 1.5 reflects, the instrumental-formal approach to symbolic action is oriented toward expectations about behavior and value as perfection in style or method (technique). The most typical activity of this cell is, of course, modern advertising, though any kind of art that becomes commodified qualifies as this kind of action. The challenge comes from artists who seek to oppose dominant forms with their artwork. Unfortunately, all such rebellions must remain small or personal, since popularity

ACTION IN THE "POLITY" VALUE SPHERE

Type of Rationality	Type of Social Action	
	Instrumental Rational Action	Value Rational Action
Formal Rationality	Political action determined by expectations and conforming to value as defined by the system of laws for insuring legitimacy and equality. For Example: - Voting in representative assemblies - Running for public office - Following parliamentary procedure - Observing legal forms	Political action determined by belief (without regard for consequences) and conforming to value as defined by the system of laws for insuring legitimacy and equality. For Example: - Voting in mass elections - Non-compulsory community service work (In a political capacity)
Substantive Rationality	Political action determined by expectations and consciously designed to be in accordance with some (non-system-based) criterion of ultimate value. For Example: - Civil disobedience - Illegal actions designed to change the law	Political action determined by belief (without regard for consequences) and consciously designed to be in accordance with some criterion of ultimate value. For Example: - Refusing to abide by laws or judgments that violate one's beliefs - Ignoring legal forms

Table 1.4 A Weberian typology of rational action and forms of rationality in the "Polity" value sphere.

undermines the force of such opposition by leading to commodification. Even the violently rebellious music of today's youth is really only a marketed rebellion and thus really no rebellion at all, since its successes are achieved through market mechanisms and consequently confirm implicitly the values of the system outwardly denounced.

In the end, this discussion about culture leaves only a paradox in its wake, but it is a paradox that affords a glimpse of the deeper, philosophical problems of modernity. Culture, according to Bell, is the sphere of human self-realization, and in modernity, "culture is defined by extraordinary freedom" (Bell: 13).   For Bell (and other neoconservatives), it is the freedom to pursue all kinds of experience for the purpose of remaking the self or achieving self-realization that strips culture of its power to affirm value.   But this is an error; the neoconservatives mistake effect for cause. Surely it is the dominance of

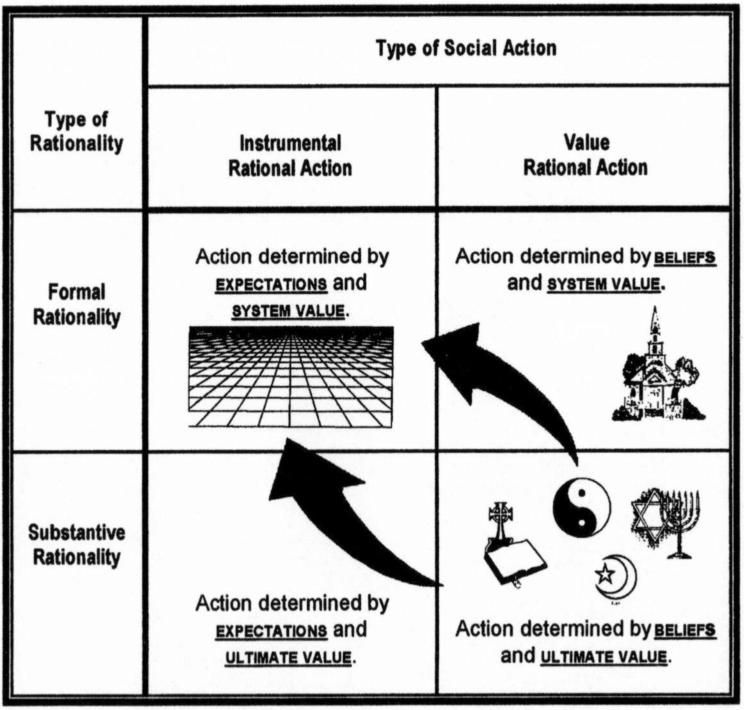

	Type of Social Action	
Type of Rationality	Instrumental Rational Action	Value Rational Action
Formal Rationality	Action determined by EXPECTATIONS and SYSTEM VALUE.	Action determined by BELIEFS and SYSTEM VALUE.
Substantive Rationality	Action determined by EXPECTATIONS and ULTIMATE VALUE.	Action determined by BELIEFS and ULTIMATE VALUE.

Figure 1-c Changes in dominance among different "types" of rationality that occur as a result of the process of rationalization.

instrumental-formal rationality in the sphere of culture that has upset the power of culture to establish value (in exactly the same way that it upset the economic and political spheres of value). The widening search for cultural "experience" as a way of achieving self-realization is clearly a reaction to the cultural situation that the rationalization process has created. The paradox is that the more vigorously people seek for new experiences in which to 'discover' themselves, the more those

ACTION IN THE "CULTURE" VALUE SPHERE

Type of Rationality	Type of Social Action	
	Instrumental Rational Action	Value Rational Action
Formal Rationality	Symbolic action determined by expectations and conforming to value as defined by systematic rules of method or style. For Example: - Television commercials and all other advertising - Popular music and film - All marketed culture & art - Political "spectacles"	Symbolic action determined by belief (without regard for consequences) and conforming to value as defined by systematic rules of method or style. For Example: - Organized prayer - Craftsmanship - Informal music groups - Chanting/Hymns - Liturgy
Substantive Rationality	Symbolic action determined by expectations and consciously designed to be in accordance with some (non-system-based) criterion of ultimate value. For Example: - Allegorical art - Evangelical art - Myths and storytelling - Some ("great" or "classic") literature - Some theater	Symbolic action determined by belief (without regard for consequences) and consciously designed to be in accordance with some (non-system-based) criterion of ultimate value. For Example: - Personal art - Self-expressive art - Musical improvisation - Personal prayer

Table 1.5 A Weberian typology of rational action and forms of rationality in the "Culture" value sphere.

experiences become commodified and lose their power to distinguish unique individuals from the general background noise of conventional, systematized society. Thus freedom comes to rule the sphere of culture, as Bell observed, yet "self" nonetheless continues to become more and more of a problem.

In summary, the fourth characteristic transformation of modernity, "rationalization," is not just 'an increase in rationality' but rather the process by which one kind of rationality, instrumental-formal rationality, becomes dominant in modern society. Through rationalization, extremely powerful self-contained and self-valuing instrumental-formal rational systems are established in modern societies. These systems change fundamentally the way most human social action is oriented in all the various "value spheres" of life and contribute greatly to the other characteristic transformations of modernity as well.

Although the achievements of rationalized modernity are undeniable even for modernity's harshest critics, the same processes that made these achievements possible are also responsible for the moral decline and social malaise discussed earlier in this chapter. Fragmentation and specialization, secularization, and the separation of the spheres were all set in motion by the Enlightenment's emphasis on the need for reason in society, and these transformations continue to be driven in great part by rationalizing tendencies today.

In the end, these trends along with the rationalization process have separated 'self' and 'system' in modern society and opposed them in such a way that 'self' may easily become overwhelmed by 'system' resulting in the kind of alienation frequently experienced by modern individuals. Consequently, society develops rapidly in its technical and organizational aspects, but remains handicapped by a weakened sense of morality and social responsibility among its members and a value system emptied of its transcendental significance and power. In short, the result is a crisis of morality caused by the struggle between 'self' and 'system' and manifesting itself in all the symptoms that are so often decried by popular critics.

1. The following discussion owes much to Philip Selznick's review of "Modernity and Modernisms" in *The Moral Commonwealth* (Selznick: 4-8).

2. The object becomes sacred in itself and the "religious forces" that are "the collective and anonymous force of the clan" come to be attributed to the totem rather than the collective will (Durkheim: 253). This is Durkheim's "totemic principle."

3. This is related to Nietzsche's well-known insight concerning science's dependence on the ascetic ideal, and its eventual confrontation with itself over the value of truth (see Nietzsche 1969: 145-156).

4. Other (non-rational) types of bases for certainty in understanding "can be of an emotionally empathic or artistically appreciative quality" (Weber 1968: 5).

5. There are actually four types of social action that Weber identifies: the two mentioned in the text plus "affectual" (including emotional) action and "traditional" (or habitual) action (Weber 1968: 24-25). These types are omitted from the present discussion because they are not rational action-orientations.

6. This equating of mathematical reason with formal rationality and logical reason with substantive rationality is actually very unclear in Weber, though I think it is a valid interpretation. Also, it should be noted that Weber tended to apply the formal-substantive distinction primarily to the "instrumental rational" category, though there is good reason to believe that he meant it to apply to both types of rational action-orientation and toward sub-categories of each type in a general sense. See Weber's *Economy and Society* (1968) pp. 4-31, 63-184, and 809-816 for original material on this subject.

CHAPTER 2

The Problems of Modernity

> *We men of knowledge of today, we godless men
> and anti-metaphysicians, we, too, still derive our
> flame from the fire ignited by a faith millennia
> old, the Christian faith, which was also Plato's,
> that God is truth, that truth is divine. —But what
> if this belief is becoming more and more
> unbelievable, if nothing turns out to be divine
> any longer unless it be error, blindness, lies—if
> God himself turns out to be our longest lie?...
> Science itself henceforth requires justification
> (which is not to say that there is any such
> justification)...*
>
> *...And here I again touch on my problem, on our
> problem... what meaning would our whole being
> possess if it were not this, that in us the will to
> truth becomes conscious of itself as a problem?*

Friedrich Nietzsche (1969: 152, 161; his italics)
On the Geneology of Morals

The characteristic transformations of modernity present the most observable evidence of modernity's impact on everyday life, but recognizing modernity's social repercussions is only the first step toward conceptualizing it well enough to deal with it as a "problem." Briefly, modernity can be understood to be a problem in three senses. At its most fundamental level the problem is philosophical, centered around what Nietzsche identified as the "ascetic ideal" inherent in modern science's "will to truth" (Nietzsche 1969: 155, 161). Yet the full implications of the problem only become apparent when modernity is approached as a cultural problem (relating to the dissolution of 'self' caused by the separation of the spheres) and as a political problem (relating to political impotence in the face of 'system' constraints).

THE PHILOSOPHICAL PROBLEM OF MODERNITY

The philosophical problem of modernity begins with what Nietzsche identifies as man's need for meaning:

> [Man] *suffered* from the problem of his meaning. He also suffered otherwise, he was in the main a sickly animal: but his problem was *not* suffering itself, but that there was no answer to the crying question, "*why* do I suffer?" (Nietzsche 1969: 162; his italics)

The answer to this question, again according to Nietzsche, was man's turn to the "ascetic ideal":

> ...The meaninglessness of suffering, *not* suffering itself, was the curse that lay over mankind so far—*and the ascetic ideal offered man meaning!* (Nietzsche 1969: 162; his italics)

The "ascetic ideal" is simply Nietzsche's way of describing any of the various routes by which people came to 'believe' their way around the 'meaninglessness' of human existence. Religious interpretations of the world are, of course, among his primary targets here, but the net is cast far and wide:

> What is the meaning of ascetic ideals? —In the case of artists they mean nothing or too many things; in the case of philosophers and scholars something like a sense and instinct for the most favorable preconditions of higher spirituality; in the case of women at best one *more* seductive charm...; in the case of the physiologically deformed and deranged (the majority of mortals) an attempt to see themselves as "too good" for this world, a saintly form of debauch, their chief weapon in the struggle against slow pain and boredom; in the case of priests the distinctive priestly faith,

> their best instrument of power, also the "supreme" license for
> power; in the case of saints, finally, a pretext for hibernation, their
> *novissima gloriae cupido* [newest lust for glory], their repose in
> nothingness ("God"), their form of madness. (Nietzsche 1969: 97;
> his italics)

In a general sense then, the ascetic ideal is (ignoring Nietzsche's
inflammatory rhetoric for the moment) whatever bestows meaning on
existence for human individuals. Something similar to this has been
offered by many as a theological definition of religion or even of
"God."[1] It should not be surprising then to find the rest of Nietzsche's
argument taking shape around the development of the principal religion
of the Western world: Christianity.

Briefly, Nietzsche depicts Christianity as having developed in three
phases—first as a dogma, then as an ethical system, and finally as
"Christian truthfulness" (by which he means "modern science"). Each
one of these phases represents a "self-overcoming" of the ascetic ideal, a
kind of Hegelian process in which the logic of one ideal gives rise to
contradictions that eventually lead to its being replaced by a new ascetic
ideal.

> In this way Christianity *as a dogma* was destroyed by its own
> morality; in the same way Christianity *as morality* must now perish,
> too: we stand on the threshold of *this* event. After Christian
> truthfulness has drawn one inference after another, it must end by
> drawing its *most striking inference*, its inference *against* itself; this
> will happen, however, when it poses the question *"what is the
> meaning of all will to truth?"* (Nietzsche 1969: 161; his italics)

It was the ethical message of Christianity itself that brought down
the dogmatic theocracy of the medieval Catholic Church, according to
Nietzsche. This ethical message was inherent within the fundamental
precepts of Christianity, even Christianity as dogmatic hierarchy. A
long line of forgotten heretics sought to exploit the innate contradiction
before Martin Luther finally initiated the reformation struggle that
would eventually bring fundamental change to the whole Christian
church. Nietzsche's argument is clear if his disturbing rhetoric is not
allowed to cloud the issue.

> Luther's attack on the mediating saints of the church (and especially
> on "the devil's sow, the pope") was, beyond any doubt,

fundamentally the attack of a lout who could not stomach the *good etiquette* of the church, that reverential etiquette of the hieratic taste which permits only the more initiated and silent into the holy of holies and closes it to louts. (Nietzsche 1969: 145; his italics)

Once again, Nietzsche goes on to argue, as the Copernican view of the universe came to be embraced by the remodeled Christian church, a new dialectical tension emerged based on ethical Christianity's immanent respect for "truth." The struggle was to work itself out over the next few centuries until modern science, Nietzsche's "Christian truthfulness," became the new standard-bearer for the ascetic ideal.

"Science today... is not the opposite of the ascetic ideal but rather *the latest and noblest form of it*" (Nietzsche 1969: 147; his italics); and scientists have not conquered the ascetic ideal—as is often contended—but rather are its most persuasive champions:

These pale atheists, anti-Christians, immoralists, nihilists... certainly believe they are as completely liberated from the ascetic ideal as possible... yet, to disclose to them what they themselves cannot see—for they are too close to themselves: this ideal is precisely *their* ideal too; they themselves embody it today and perhaps they alone; they themselves are its most spiritualized product, its most advanced front-line troops and scouts, its most captious, tender, intangible form of seduction... They are far from being *free* spirits: *for they still have faith in truth.* (Nietzsche 1969: 149-150; his italics)

Even scientific atheism does not escape the ascetic ideal:

Unconditional honest atheism... is therefore *not* the antithesis of that ideal, as it appears to be; it is rather only one of the latest phases of its evolution, one of its terminal forms and inner consequences—it is the awe-inspiring *catastrophe* of two thousand years of training in truthfulness that finally forbids itself the *lie involved in belief in God.* (Nietzsche 1969: 160; his italics)

Nietzsche goes on to note how the life-denying quality of the ascetic ideal is admirably and ostentatiously displayed by science:

Physiologically, too, science rests on the same foundation as the ascetic ideal: a certain *impoverishment of life* is a presupposition of both of them—the affects grown cool, the tempo of life slowed

down, dialectics in place of instinct, seriousness imprinted on faces
and gestures... A predominance of mandarins always means
something is wrong...

Has the self-belittlement of man, his *will* to self-belittlement, not
progressed irresistibly since Copernicus? Alas, the faith in the
dignity and uniqueness of man, in his irreplaceability in the great
chain of being, is a thing of the past—he has become an *animal*,
literally and without reservation or qualification, he who was,
according to his old faith, almost God...

Since Copernicus, man seems to have got himself on an inclined
plane—now he is slipping faster and faster away from the center
into—what? into nothingness? into a *"penetrating* sense of his
nothingness"? Very well! hasn't this been the straightest route to—
the *old* [ascetic] ideal?...

All science... has at present the object of dissuading man from his
former respect for himself. (Nietzsche 1969: 154-156: his italics)

Originally, the ascetic ideal had been created to escape the
meaninglessness of suffering. Through devotion to this ideal, the
ascetic interpreted his suffering and made it bearable, even something to
be desired. At the same time, however, the ascetic ideal negated passion
and spirit, substituting a dispassionate aloofness for the elemental
furnace that was life between exaltation and despair. But the antiseptic
quality of this withdrawal from the world (and here is found the actual
target of all Nietzsche's rhetoric) resulted not only in the minimization of
pain and the realization of social progress, but also in the weakening of
human spirit.

With Nietzsche, it became clear that the general trend of modernity
was not only to minimize the suffering in life, but actually to escape life
itself. The suffering that comes with exaltation and despair is, after all,
an important part of living, especially with regard to the meaning people
attach to living.

We can no longer conceal from ourselves *what* is expressed by all
that willing which has taken its direction from the ascetic ideal: this
hatred of the human... this fear of happiness and beauty, this longing
to get away from all appearance, change, becoming, death, wishing,
from longing itself—all this means—let us dare to grasp It—a *will*
to nothingness, an aversion to life, a rebellion against the most

fundamental presuppositions of life; but... man would rather will *nothingness* than *not* will. (Nietzsche 1969: 162-163; his italics)

Modernity—as a lifestyle based on modern science, reason, and the pursuit of truth—is thus, in Nietzsche's words, "a will to nothingness," a culture placed in opposition to life. This is the fundamental logic underlying the problem of modernity: modernity is a form of life in opposition to life; it saves people from despair, but only at the cost of their humanity. Philosophically, it is self-contradictory in that it demands that people become something they are not in order to be better what they are.

All this is revealed in the final act of "self-overcoming" of the ascetic ideal in the modern world. Christian truthfulness (modern science) must, like dogmatic Christianity and ethical Christianity, also confront its immanent contradictions in a process of unfolding. But the consequences of modern science's inward turn are unique:

> We men of knowledge of today, we godless men and anti-metaphysicians, we, too, still derive *our* flame from the fire ignited by a faith millennia old, the Christian faith, which was also Plato's, that God is truth, that truth is *divine*. —But what if this belief is becoming more and more unbelievable, if nothing turns out to be divine any longer unless it be error, blindness, lies—if God himself turns out to be our *longest lie?*
>
> ...Science itself henceforth *requires* justification (which is not to say that there is any such justification)...
>
> After Christian truthfulness has drawn one inference after another, it must end by drawing its *most striking inference*, its inference *against* itself; this will happen, however, when it poses the question *"what is the meaning of all will to truth?"*
> And here I again touch on my problem, on our problem... what meaning would *our* whole being possess if it were not this, that in us the will to truth becomes conscious of itself as a *problem?* (Nietzsche 1969: 152, 161; his italics)

The problem that the unfolding or "self-overcoming" of modern science leaves for modern individuals is the threat of an impending loss of meaning brought on by the self-destruction of the ascetic ideal—in a word, nihilism. However one chooses to interpret Nietzsche's use of the word "God" throughout this argument, his statement remains one of the most forceful presentations of the problem of modernity to this day. Indeed, his forecast for the twentieth century sounds eerily contemporary:

> As the will to truth thus gains self-consciousness—there can be no doubt of that—morality will gradually *perish* now: this is the great spectacle in a hundred acts reserved for the next two centuries in Europe—the most terrible, most questionable, and perhaps also the most hopeful of all spectacles. (Nietzsche 1969: 161; his italics)

THE CULTURAL PROBLEM OF MODERNITY

The cultural problem of modernity has its origins in the Enlightenment's turn to reason and humanism as the basis for a new style of living. This may be difficult to see at first. The Enlightenment was in many respects a time when the best of humanity flourished, but the ultimate cultural implications of the Enlightenment's emphasis on reason become much harder to overlook following the advent of capitalism and the coming of the information revolution.

Modern culture—the culture of capitalist economics, mass society and computer information technology—has become a cult of reason and efficiency. It overshadows people's lives every bit as fatefully as the Papacy ever did, but the modern economy offers no more spiritual assistance than Rome did technical. The inescapable fact of having to live in such a culture has loomed over the thought of every major social theorist since Nietzsche. Most sought to understand the problem through what they characterized as the "pathologies" of modern life. For Marx this meant 'alienation,' for Durkheim 'anomie,' for Freud 'discontent,' for others 'leveling,' 'disenchantment,' 'domination,' 'rationalization,' and so on. But the origin of all of these "pathologies," as most knew, is modern culture beginning with the constricting force of what Weber termed the "iron cage" (Weber 1958: 181).

According to Weber (and following Nietzsche), the "iron cage" of modern culture begins with the religious ascetic's appropriation of reason as the basis for the "ascetic ideal." This ideal bridged the chasm between spiritual perfection in one's relationship with God and perfection in one's in-this-worldly behavior, especially as such behavior related to discipline and devotion to duty:

Asceticism emphasizes non-material values, renunciation of physical pleasures, simplicity and self-denial, and arduous, purposeful discipline. That discipline is necessary for the mobilization of psychic and physical energies for tasks outside the self, for the conquest and subordination of the self in order to conquer others. (Bell: 82)

Protestantism and finally Puritanism extended this concept to work in a "vocation," effectively making economic success a sign of ardent devotion to God. In terms of Weber's typologies of rationality and rational social action, the Puritans introduced formal rationality to value-rational economic social action (see figure 2-a). Here, in Weber's

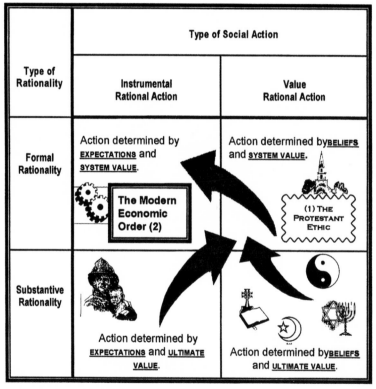

Figure 2-a: The unification of formal rationality and value-rational economic social action in the "Protestant ethic" (1) leading to the modern economic order (2).

upper right-hand cell, the formal rules of the economic system are taken as a measure of success (or failure) in the spiritual realm.

But this vocational ethos (Weber's "Protestant ethic") is eventually "overcome... by the material powers of capitalist development" (Scaff: 88). Essentially, vocational activity begins to take on a life of its own, independent of the Puritan ideal, until the "ethic" of vocational discipline is forgotten and only simple acquisitiveness remains. Now action shifts to the upper-left cell of Weber's typology, uniting formal rationality and instrumental rational social action together in the modern rational economic order (figure 2-a). But once this unity is achieved, the competitive logic of modern capitalism takes over and the system is driven forward of its own accord without the necessary impetus of any human 'will'.

Instead of being industrious for God, people begin to work diligently for their own (hedonistic) reasons. Goods (money, commodities, social status, etc.) replace God as the driving force of modern entrepreneurial efficiency and rational administration. For the modern individual, the consequences of this change are universal and inescapable:

> The Puritan *wanted* to work in a vocation [*wollte Berufsmensch sein*]; we *must* do so. For when asceticism was carried out of monastic cells into vocational life and began to dominate inner-worldly morality, it helped to build the tremendous cosmos of the modern economic order. This order is now bound to the technical and economic presuppositions of mechanical, machinelike production, which today determines with irresistible force the lifestyle [*Lebensstil*] of all individuals born into this mechanism, *not* only those directly engaged in economic enterprise, and perhaps will determine it until the last ton of fossil coal is burned. (Weber, quoted and translated in Scaff: 88)

It was the Puritan's ethic of diligent work that set modern economic rationalism in motion. But where the Puritan's motive was always essentially spiritual, there is no use for such motives in the secular form of life practiced in modernity.

> In Baxter's view the care for external goods should only lie on the shoulders of the saint like "a light cloak, which can be thrown aside at any moment." But fate [*Verhängnis*] decreed that the cloak

should become an iron cage. (Weber, quoted and translated in Scaff: 88).

The "iron cage" of the vocational/commodity culture of advanced capitalism, however, is only the first dimension of the cultural problem of modernity. Just as important is the moral vacuum left after the Protestant ethic is overwhelmed. When vocational activity is "stripped of its sustaining structures of meaning" (Scaff: 88), the result is a culture unable to assign value in any ultimate sense. It is this condition, together with the growing dominance of formal-instrumental rational action in economic affairs, which allows for "the separation of the spheres" to occur. Since the greater culture is unable to assign any comprehensive social value, lesser cultures develop around the fragmented experiences of modern life. Of course, a society in which there is no greater culture capable of establishing values that transcend experience is also, by definition, a society in moral crisis (in Durkheim's sense—see pp. 9-10).

The most important problem that arises from the separation of the spheres is more significant for individuals than for society at large. Following the explosion of value-spheres appearing after the demise of unified central culture, the "self" becomes problematic for individuals. As people move from sphere to sphere (work to family to politics, for example), they must submit themselves to the imperatives of different value realms—imperatives which, more often than not, demand contradictory self-understandings from individuals. It is no wonder that one's sense of "self" becomes more and more confused in this process.

The confusion in the "self" is mitigated only by its fundamental enmity with formal systems and particularly by its enmity with the formal-rational sphere of economic action. Substantive forms are more conducive than formal systems to the life of the self because formal systems obliterate the unique qualities of individuals in order to level them into categorical classes. Such treatment makes the abuse of individual differences standard operating procedure and cannot fail to injure or at least antagonize the independence and confidence of the self. Such antagonism is commonly experienced, for example, when dealing with bureaucracies (in which individuals are 'processed' according to fixed rules) and in the marketplace (where one's labor, even one's 'value,' is quantified to fit an economic scale).

The clash that reveals the true depth of the cultural problem of modernity comes when the self, weakened by the separation of the spheres but maintaining its animosity toward formal systems, comes head to head with the awesome power of the modern economic system. Now all three elements of the "cultural problem of modernity"—the iron cage of modern capitalism, the separation of the spheres, and the animosity between self and system—explode in a reaction that triggers the "pathologies of modern culture." "Anomie," "alienation," and "disenchantment" rise as the 'self' becomes frustrated and attenuated in its struggle to escape the system imperatives of modern capitalism—or rather, as people's awareness of the continuing diminution of the importance of self in modern society increases. Simply put, the problem is that modern culture *forces* people to live the lifestyle of acquisitive capitalism, while at the same time judging this form of life to be spiritually unrewarding, morally empty, and ultimately worthless.

This recognition reveals the full importance of Weber's image of the iron cage. It is not just that people are bound into the rigors of modern economic life, but that they are bound into them absent the human qualities that redeem the tedium and futility of the daily struggle for survival: with full knowledge of the loss. As for those who proudly revel in this spiritual wasteland (the Faustian champions of development and 'progress') Weber's words are perhaps still the most telling:

> For the "ultimate beings" of this cultural development it might well be truly said: "specialists without spirit, sensualists without heart: this nullity imagines that it has attained a level of civilization (*Menschentum*) never before achieved." (Hennis: 153, quoting Weber)

In the end, Weber's condemnation of the iron cage, and indeed the whole thesis against the culture of modernity, is grounded in a rejection of the intolerable conditions imposed by modern culture on the human spirit.

THE POLITICAL PROBLEM OF MODERNITY

The political problem of modernity follows naturally from the problem of modern culture. The crux of the matter is how to reassert effectively the power of the human spirit in modern culture. Any worthy solution would have to refocus the confidence of the self in its own identity (overcoming the problem posed by the separation of the spheres in some way) and strengthen the arenas of substantive forms of rationality enough to achieve a more equal balance with the formal-rational systems of modernity. The prospects for such a solution are not hopeful, but a few leads are available, some even inherent in the culture of modernity itself.

The first possibility, which must be rejected, is to look to the past. It is true that modernity appears to 'lessen' a quality that humans think they once possessed, but there is no going back to the spirituality of pre-modern times. To do so would be to abandon all the achievements of modernity (including the wonders of modern science) and, even more importantly, to sacrifice the human intellect on an altar of self-deceit. For those who have embraced modernity (or had it thrust upon them) and who would remain intellectually honest about the experience, the door to the old forms of spiritual self-identity must remain closed forever. This was the meaning of Nietzsche's peremptory declaration that "God is Dead" (Nietzsche 1974: 125).

Nevertheless, God is more wily and subtle than Nietzsche's requiem admits. Returning to the past is certainly not possible, but the seeds of a renewed presence for the human spirit may have been sewn as early as the Enlightenment.

While it is true that the Enlightenment marked the beginning of rationalizing influences in Western culture, it also marked the advent of certain "deliberative ideals" in political thought. Political equality and democracy (as substantive political ideals) are concepts that directly challenge all of the characteristic trends of modernity. The basis of their challenge is the value they place on human community and the protection of the unique individual qualities over and above concerns about efficiency and administrative excellence.

For example, the modern tendency to promote fragmentation is discouraged by (substantive) democracy's emphasis on the value of community. Specialization is tempered by political equality's insistence on the equal importance of all citizens (regardless of the presence of qualitative inequalities between unique individuals). The instrumental-rational demand for economic efficiency is countered by a contrasting overall emphasis on political accommodation. Even the trend toward secularization is countered by commitment to the ideals of democracy and equality. (Note that "commitment" implies value-content and, consequently, substantive rather than empirically rational foundations.) Most important, it seems clear that in modernity, the "human spirit" comes to achieve its fullest expression in the communities where these ideals are actively pursued by each member?

Of course, whether simple commitment to the political ideals of democracy and political equality could effectively either empower the self or combat the formal-rational forms of modern society is doubtful. The problem is that modern culture has eclipsed the deliberative ideals of political equality and democracy since the Enlightenment, and never more completely than in recent years. The dominance of formal-instrumental rationality in modernity gives rise to economic patterns that prevent equality and a technical mindset that encourages administrative solutions to political problems. In essence, the technical ideals of enlightenment, exalted by modern culture and made requisite by mass society, have come to dominate the deliberative ones. The political problem of modernity then must be to find ways of reasserting the power of those deliberative ideals within the suffocating atmosphere of modern culture.

----

1. One excellent example is Paul Tillich's *Dynamics of Faith* (Tillich, 1957).

2. It is interesting to note that in recent years many religious communities have adjusted to the needs of modern people to such an extent that the values of equality, democracy, and community have become the agreed standard for practical association. Increasingly, these ideals are also coming to be expressed as matters of faith. (Durkheim might even judge them "sacred" in the sense that they are becoming symbols of communities' self-identity.) This may sound surprising, but after reflection it should not be. The fundamental messages of many world religions focus on community. Why couldn't democracy and political equality come to characterize some of these associations in the same way that Nietzsche saw dogma, ethics, and truth as characterizing the Christian church through recent ages? Indeed, if the basis for future spirituality is to be found in the practice of community, then churches might be uniquely positioned to encourage this trend in modern society.

CHAPTER 3

Modernity in the Context of Human Struggle

> *Life is, in itself and forever, shipwreck. To be shipwrecked is not to drown. The poor human being, feeling himself sinking into the abyss, moves his arms to keep afloat. This movement of the arms which is his reaction against his own destruction, is culture—a swimming stroke—. When culture is no more than this, it fulfills its function and the human being rises above his own abyss.*[1]
>
> José Ortega y Gasset (1956: 126)
> "In Search of Goethe from Within"

European political theorists have been discussing the characteristic trends of modernity and the problem of modernity in all three of its aspects for many years. Their conclusions would fill many volumes, and the strategies they offer to resist the tide of modern influences range widely—from stoic discipline to social constructions based on idealized speech to enthusiastic pursuit of art, experience, eroticism, and other sanctuaries. But the European understanding of the problem of modernity is limited to a perspective based on European experience. Authors with different historical experiences also have much to say about the subject and much to add to the general understanding of modernity.

Latin America is in a unique position in relation to modernity. Like many less developed regions, it supports a traditional culture facing imminent modernization and development. Few nations of the world exist so directly in the shadow of modernity as the peoples living south of the United States in the Western Hemisphere. American culture constantly subjects Mexico to an intense barrage of modern influences, and the rest of Latin America receives the same treatment, made only slightly less intense by the factor of distance. These Latin American communities are microcosms of the clashes that characterize the transition to modernity in general: old vs. new, European vs. Indian, soldier vs. farmer, television vs. storyteller, etc.

It is true that many less developed regions of the world share at least some important characteristics with Latin America but, unlike other regions Latin America is home to an intellectual community that is well versed in the problems of modern life. Latin American intellectuals, cued by their European literary and philosophical heritage, have paid considerable attention to the problem of modernity. Thus Latin American culture is sufficiently different from that of Europe to present a distinct encounter with modernity, but not so different as to be uninstructive. European theorists, for example, tend to write as if looking back on a transition to modernity that continues to pattern their experience while the Latin American time perspective is more immediate. Latin authors write as if riding the floodwater of modernity instead of surveying its damage or charting its currents. The European approach to modernity is also different in that it is disproportionately analytical, highlighting the economic and sociopolitical consequences of modernity over the personal, emotional, and spiritual concerns that are of central importance to Latin American authors. Clearly, there is much to learn from a serious consideration of the Latin American understanding of modernity.

JOSÉ ORTEGA Y GASSET

José Ortega y Gasset, the great Spanish writer and philosopher of the early twentieth century, revitalized Spanish philosophy during his prolific career and at the same time introduced Latin American intellectuals to contemporary European social thought. His work presented the understanding of modernity that would become paradigmatic for generations of Latin American authors and social critics. It would also set the tone for a distinct new philosophical response to the problems of modernity outlined in the previous chapter.

Ortega received his doctorate in 1904 and spent the next five years studying in Germany, where he gained a thorough knowledge of German philosophy. After returning to Spain in 1910 to become professor of metaphysics at the University of Madrid, he became active in journalism and politics as well as philosophy. Although prolific in writing essays and articles of general cultural interest, Ortega wrote fewer strictly philosophical works. Instead, his impact on Spanish philosophy was strongest in his role as teacher and critic, a style that seems appropriate for one who found "life" (as the career and destiny of an individual within society and history) to be the touchstone of ultimate reality (Dobson: 112-114).

Ortega sought to move beyond both idealism and realism in his philosophy by asserting that self and things are constitutive of each other and neither one should be considered prior to or dependent on the other. "I am I and my circumstances" (*Yo soy Yo y mi circunstancia*) was his most famous summation of this idea (Gray: 187-189). This understanding of man as an individual within historical context is present throughout Ortega's philosophy. With regard to knowledge, Ortega emphasized that the world could only be known from one's own particular point of view, and that "the only false perspective is the one that claims to be the one and only perspective" (Ortega quoted in McInnes: 3). Ethically, Ortega considered the responsible person to be the one committed to a life project or vocation while immorality consisted in allowing oneself to be swept along by transient circumstances: the failure to pursue a personal destiny.[2]

The understanding of people as both self and circumstance comes together with Ortega's ethical thought to make a fascinating existentialist philosophy. Life is seen to present people with a continuous barrage of choices, and people, through their exercise of reason, create their own personality by making those choices. Thus life has a purpose or goal in the building of character through the exercise of human reason. "It is by intelligent reckoning with his circumstances that a man gains his being and becomes himself" (McInnes: 4).

Ortega's philosophy of culture also incorporates his perspectivism, and it is probably the area of his thought most relevant to the theme of modernity. Ortega described culture variously as "the essential system of ideas concerning the world and man which belong to our time," "the system of ideas by which an age conducts its life," and "our active convictions as to the nature of our world and our fellow creatures" (Ortega, quoted in Kerr: 81). He always presents culture in dynamic terms and as situated within an historical context. While it is true that many others have characterized culture in similar ways, for Ortega culture is unusually important. In his philosophy it is, after all, only culture that allows humanity to forge the oppressions of life into a dignified expression of human spirit. If moral life is dedication to a project or vocation, then culture is the "essential system of ideas" out of which individuals may put together "projects" and "vocations" appropriate to the time. Thus for Ortega, culture becomes both the hope of the individual and the highest expression of collective human dignity.

As for the problem of modernity, Ortega essentially adopted the same conception of the problem that was originally put forward by Nietzsche and later accepted by other European social theorists. Nevertheless, his philosophy of culture lead him to promote a significantly different response to the problem.

According to Ortega y Gasset, life is and has always been a tragedy, a "shipwreck." In the case of the present age, Ortega agrees that the problem of modernity is ethical in nature—a crisis of morality. "Vital disorientation" is the term he uses to describe the phenomenon, clearly referring to modernity as a cultural problem. Weber would have called it "disenchantment," but the meaning is the same:

> The system of values by which [modern people's] activity was regulated thirty years ago has lost its convincing character, its attractive force and its imperative vigor. The man of the West is undergoing a process of radical disorientation because he no longer knows by what stars he is to guide his life. (Ortega y Gasset, 1961: 79)

Thus Ortega is essentially in agreement with Weber and the German theorists concerning the cultural problem of modernity. His praise of Nietzsche as one of the "seers of genius" who uncovered the basic problem of values in modern society also leaves little doubt about his acceptance of the Central European conception of modernity as a philosophical problem (Ortega y Gasset, 1961: 78).

Despite substantial agreement about the nature of the problem, Ortega also refined the German conception of modernity to fit his own (Latin) style. One subtle, but important difference is apparent in the way in which he presents the character of modernity. For Ortega, the loss of value foundations in modernity is a lively process, devoid of the "unnatural" quality present in German warnings about nihilism and 'the abyss':

> A life, then, which finds the exercise of its own powers more interesting and valuable than the prosecution of those aims which the taste of yesteryear garnished with so unique a prestige will give to its efforts the cheerful, hearty and even slightly waggish air that is peculiar to sport... It will create its splendors as if in jest, and will not endow them with any great importance. The poet will manage his art with his toes, like a good footballer. (Ortega y Gasset 1961: 83)

By Ortega's view, the attitude toward "life" expressed in this passage goes on to set up an important contradiction between relativism (evident in life lived with the attitude of sport, as expressed above) and rationalism (in which the importance of unified culture is primary). This point will become important later for understanding Ortega's response to the problem of modernity. For now, it is sufficient to note that Ortega's emphasis on "life" gives his conception of modernity a far different character than the dismal one commonly presented by other European theorists.

A second, more important, way in which Ortega refines the standard conception of modernity is to displace the German emphasis on the constricting structure of modern culture. In particular, Weber's image of the "iron cage" of modern capitalist culture seems to have fallen out of Ortega's account. Indeed, where Weber saw the culture of acquisitive capitalism as the force that condemns people in modernity to a disenchanted existence, Ortega sees culture itself as the means, not of escape, exactly, but of confronting and surviving (with spirit intact) the flood of modernity.

One way to understand how Ortega is able to avoid Weber's discouraging conclusion about modern culture is to consider the very different conceptions each man had about the underlying nature of the problem. For Weber, the culture of modern capitalism developed out of an entirely new, never-before-encountered chain of events. As such, the crisis of modernity is for Weber a unique event, as new and unstoppable to modern man as smallpox was to the native cultures of America. But for Ortega, the crisis of modernity is not a unique event in the history of humanity. On the contrary, it is only the demon of the current generation, the most recent of the continuing series of historical catastrophes that define human existence.

For José Ortega y Gasset, catastrophe is the defining moment of human life from which all else must proceed. People not only have a stubborn capacity to rise above the tragedy of their circumstances and forge a dignified existence amid the chaos of life, but they are also seen to be at their best when engaged in this struggle. Thus for Ortega the problem of modernity is neither the unique event it was for Weber, nor the suffocating and inescapable "iron cage."

> Life is, in itself and forever, shipwreck. To be shipwrecked is not to drown. The poor human being, feeling himself sinking into the abyss, moves his arms to keep afloat. This movement of the arms which is his reaction against his own destruction, is culture—a swimming stroke—. When culture is no more than this, it fulfills its function and the human being rises above his own abyss. (Ortega y Gasset, 1956: 126)

Thus for Ortega, culture is not only the problem in modernity but also the solution. It is the creative, sustaining swimming power that keeps people from sinking beneath the waves. To be shipwrecked, as with the problem of modernity, is *not* to drown: "Ortega holds that this poor shipwrecked humanity can learn to swim, that is, that it possesses the requisite ability to learn how to confront and resolve, at least in part, the crisis which threatens its existence" (Dust: 305). Indeed, Ortega believed that "history... is filled with examples of... improbable recoveries" from such crises, and that the means of recovery so decisive in such circumstances has always been the human capacity to reinvent and adapt "culture." By Ortega's view, humanity has been continually confronting and resolving such crises—treading water—since the beginning of history, and he clearly considered the problem of the current age to be "one more manifestation of the same phenomenon" (Dust: 299).

Ortega's refinements of the standard approach to modernity are thus significant, but his disagreements with Weber only set the stage for continuing differences on the issue of the proper response to the crisis of modernity. Though the essential problem remains the same, Ortega's advice concerning "the task of our time" is unique among the alternatives commonly put forward by other philosophers. Competing responses to the crisis of modernity include at least three popular approaches that offer prescriptions fundamentally different from Ortega's: "modernism," "post-modernism," and "neo-conservatism."[3]

COMPETING RESPONSES TO THE CRISIS OF MODERNITY

Modernism developed in the mid-nineteenth century as the social pressures of modernity grew intense. As a response to the value crisis of modernity, modernism retained much of the Enlightenment's confidence in reason and progress, but it became a confidence tempered by a new appreciation for subjectivity, perspectivism, and the loss of stabilizing beliefs and meaningful order.

Despite the deeply troubling impact of these developments, modernism's first achievement was to transform the shock of discovery into an enthusiastic release of creative energy. Innovation came to be seen as its own reward. Art, architecture, science, and many other aspects of social life experienced rapid change and adopted radical new directions as a result of the modernist drive to question and tear down old ways of doing things and quickly erect new constructions in their place. But though modernism's constant innovation and change proved a comforting diversion for nearly a century, eventually it would lead to fatigue and finally exhaustion. Without the direction and temperance provided by an underlying normative foundation, "progress" was achieved everywhere without ever adding up to anything meaningful. By the mid-twentieth century the open and forward-looking attitude of modernism had burnt itself out, and the underlying problems of subjectivity and ethical uncertainty became more compelling than ever before.

Modernism remains an important response to the changed social conditions of modernity but without the allure it once possessed. Today modernism is most often encountered as an unsophisticated faith in progress, but even in its more advanced forms modernism suffers from an inability to recognize the dangers inherent in failing to confront the underlying ethical crisis of modernity. It overlooks what José Ortega y Gasset understood to be the basic human condition: shipwreck. One does not escape shipwreck by ignoring a breached hull or erecting an impressive new superstructure. Besides increasing the risk of total catastrophe (as in nuclear war, for example), modernism simply does not recognize the ongoing damage that unconsidered faith in "the new" presents to human character. Applied technology may continue to provide us with better ways to feed and divert the multitudes, but it will never, in itself, help us to be better people. Like a drug, modernism diverts people from considering the real ethical problems of living life in our time. It mistakenly elevates technological innovation to the place where cultural renewal should be, and so substitutes progress for struggle, emptiness for fullness, and death for life.

Postmodernism, a second response to the changed social conditions in modernity, gathered strength as the influence of modernism declined. Postmodernism takes the shattered ethical landscape as its central insight and "celebrates the latent nihilism in the modernist outlook" (Selznick: 9). All truth is contextual for postmodernism, and therefore no single "objective" truth is possible. Furthermore, since every perspective, every truth, must be biased in some way, it must also be possible to uncover that bias and lay bare the underlying power relationships that created it. In this way the modern penchant for destruction before reconstruction becomes the postmodern thirst for "deconstruction": the uncovering of power relationships latent within social forms.[4]

While Ortega would not disagree with the basic insight that all truth is contextual and perspective-bound, he would certainly take issue with postmodernism's radical conclusion that cultural forms should be deconstructed and new truths not be sought. The postmodern argument is that since human knowledge is by nature context-bound and incommensurable, people must learn to enjoy existence in the fragmented world of disconnected "language games" that modernity has become (see Lyotard, 1984). To try to build greater cultural truths would be to introduce power relationships that surely would be biased against some groups and in favor of others.

But such an acceptance of the loss of unified culture would be anathema to José Ortega y Gasset. To give up on culture would be for the poor shipwrecked soul to quit swimming and drown. Thus for Ortega, postmodernism is the embracing of nihilism and the murder of culture. Even though he fully accepts the postmodern insight of perspectivism, Ortega denies its radical stand against culture as unnecessary. Relativism may be a fact of modern life, but that alone does not warrant abandoning the effort to create a consistent ethical system within human culture, any more than the fact of human mortality warrants suicide (or despair).

Thus while it is true that postmodernism does not suffer from the same blindness toward cultural deterioration that modernism does, the other limitations of the approach are if anything even more problematic. Postmodernists, for all their deconstructive acumen, are no more able to support a renewed moral/ethical order than the modernists. Indeed, according to postmodern thought, even the attempt to do so would be considered counterproductive. Thus postmodernism is unable to build and unable to offer humanity any future other than an endless wallowing in dismal, hopeless nihilism.

Neoconservatism is the third fashionable response to modernity. Daniel Bell's *The Cultural Contradictions of Capitalism* is perhaps the most well-known and well-respected statement of this response to modernity (Bell, 1976). It begins with a forceful critique of modernism, claiming that modern culture has lead to hedonism and rebellion against authority in the common people; such an attitude ultimately gave rise to the moral crisis of modernity.[5]

According to Bell, the advent of modern capitalism first undermined the traditional value system by setting up a hedonistic system of rewards to compete with the old theological justifications for hard work and dedication. Profit, and the pleasure that comes of it, eventually replaced God as the motive force behind the pursuit of progress but was unable to endow work with the depth of meaning and social responsibility that curbed human excesses in earlier times. The result was a radically undirected culture that promoted the pursuit of progress without regard to where it might lead. Thus, by Bell's way of thinking, it is the shallowness of modern culture that makes people lose their grip on the moral/ethical foundations of society.[6]

The neoconservative response to this situation is exactly opposite what postmodernism advocates. Instead of accepting the fragmented, valueless world of the modern (or postmodern), Bell would have people return to the security of a religious outlook on the world.

"Hubris" is the central issue here, according to Bell. People must recognize that life is insecure and the world far more powerful than humanity, even a humanity armed with the toys of technology (perhaps especially so). To remedy the situation, people need to accept the fact that they must reach beyond themselves; only a new revelation can succeed in both reuniting the fragmented and divided culture of modernity and establishing a common ethical foundation for society.

While Ortega would certainly agree with Bell's diagnosis of the culture of modernity, he would also denounce the American sociologist's turn to religion as a misguided hope for *deus ex machina*. In effect, the neoconservative response to modernity is similar to the postmodern attempt to escape from culture in the sense that it too would have poor shipwrecked humanity abandon the effort to stay above the waves. The difference is that instead of claiming that humanity should enjoy drowning (as postmodernism does), the neoconservative response would simply have humanity stop swimming and look to the sky for rescue.

Ortega's Response to the problems of modernity is not concerned with whether or not the rescue hoped for by neoconservatives is possible or likely. Instead, the issue becomes one of responsibility. For Ortega, it would be irresponsible for humanity to stop its own efforts to stay alive whether or not rescue is possible. This position has the triple virtue of being a viable response whether or not religion has a role to play in the salvation of humanity, coming entirely from within the human condition and looking to the future of culture rather than toward any return to "the sacred" (Bell: 171).

Ortega y Gasset's response to the crisis of modernity, while by no means the final word on the subject, does manage to avoid the worst offenses of the responses already discussed. Modernism fails because it does not recognize the fragility of the human condition and the danger presented to society by unbridled "progress." Postmodernism recognizes the bounds of human knowledge and progress but rejects any effort to build renewed cultural and ethical foundations. Finally neoconservatism, though it recognizes both the need to put limits on progress and the demand for a coherent ethical sphere, does not put forward a viable *human* strategy for confronting the perils of modernity.

Ortega's philosophy avoids all of these difficulties without being radically different (in its understanding of the problem of modernity) from any of the other approaches. His success stems from what he would surely consider his most fundamental insight: that "life is, in itself and forever, shipwreck" (Ortega, 1956: 397). Once this essential starting point is accepted, the rest of his interpretation of "the task of our time" unfolds with logical precision.

"The first thing that must be done, however, is to *accept* the current situation for what it is: a terrible disaster with a potential for bringing about the complete destruction of our planet" (Dust: 305). For Ortega, the shipwreck of life always threatens to bring an end to human society as it is known irrespective of historical setting, and nuclear arms are just another manifestation of that threat (albeit a very powerful one). What is imperative is that people somehow gain the courage to accept the threat as real and become fully engaged in the struggle to put off the impending doom.

> The important thing to see here is that this acceptance and this courage do not take place in any imaginary realm and that they do not involve the timely intervention of superhuman forces. They occur completely within history, within this flawed and struggling dimension of human society, where man creates values which are imperfect but still genuine values nonetheless. This is what Nietzsche would call a human, all too human, drama, and if our true situation is to be accepted, it entails accepting this as well. Ortega is explicit about this, emphasizing above all an extraordinary capacity for embracing our situation, "gladly, in all its effective reality." Only after taking this step does he believe we can turn our attention to the possibility of realistically improving the situation. (Dust: 307).

The specific peril that nuclear weapons represent in the image taken from Patrick Dust and in Ortega y Gasset's philosophy is the same cultural problem of modernity that has been consistently recognized by all of modernity's critics; progress (and especially technological progress) is moving forward at a rapid pace while society's cultural and ethical foundations are disintegrating almost as quickly. Once this peril is recognized for the existential threat that Ortega describes, it becomes possible for him to define more specifically "the task of our time."

Ortega sets his explanation in terms of a confrontation between "rationalism" (objectivism) and "relativism." In modernity, he says, "life" comes to be pitted against "culture" as postmodern relativism makes inroads against modern rationalism. "Rationalism... in its design to preserve culture denies all significance to life," and "relativism... attempts [to get] rid of the objective value of culture altogether in order to leave room for life" (Ortega y Gasset, 1961: 86). At issue here, among other things, is foundational ethics. "Rationalists" would have a unified ethical sphere in culture while "relativists" would denounce such a foundational construction as an unacceptable imposition of one point of view on everyone. Rationalists deny "life" by seeking to exclude nonconforming viewpoints, while relativists sacrifice cultural and ethical consistency by seeking to preserve the integrity of all points-of view. But neither one of these alternatives is acceptable to Ortega because both cultural consistency and life (or "vitality") are necessary to have a healthy society. "Our own age... cannot bring itself either to accept the idea that truth, justice and beauty do not exist, or to forget that their existence requires the support of vitality" (Ortega y Gasset, 1961: 87). Without a vigorous effort to posit consistent cultural and ethical ideas (like justice and beauty) across society, values will lose their meaning and society will experience a crisis that could lead to its being smothered in a sea of empty values. Similarly, without the constant testing of social values and ongoing pursuit of new ideas, cultural constructions will lose their meaning and become hollow, resulting in the same cultural asphyxiation. Thus for Ortega the "task of our time" must be to overcome the division between these two perspectives.

It is not difficult to see the parallels between "rationalism" and modernism, and "relativism" and postmodernism. The critique given above could be easily applied to modernism and postmodernism. Clearly, Ortega sees a need to overcome the limitations of these responses.

The answer is found in Ortega's unique interpretation of the nature of the problem of modernity. Recall that for Ortega all human life is crisis, and humans are equipped to deal with their crises at least well enough to stay afloat, even if no permanent "solution" is forthcoming. Clearly Ortega is saying that both cultural consistency and perspectivist vitality are necessary responses to modernity. More than that, he is also saying that to go too far either toward rationalism (and modernism) or relativism (and postmodernism) is to invite failure. Indeed, according to this reading, by advocating one approach to the exclusion of the other both the modernists and the postmodernists are leading society to drowning: the one by exhaustion, the other by hypothermia. Instead, society should recognize that the proper response to modernity is to attempt to achieve balance by keeping some measure of culture alive in all of its aspects—to delight in life by relishing whatever small successes are manifest in the cultural achievements of the day.

Ortega's response goes beyond Bell and the neoconservatives by encouraging an active human response to the crisis of modernity without falling prey to the hubris that Bell was so keen to avoid. Poor shipwrecked humanity must actively try to stay afloat or it will sink beneath the waves. There is no hubris in treading water, and Ortega never suggests that humanity will be able to walk on it. All solutions will be partial at best, so humanity should be well aware of its limitations. In any case, simply waiting for a new revelation, as the neoconservatives advocate, will not do the job. Even if salvation were to come in such a dramatic fashion, the swimmer would surely drown before its arrival without first making the all too human effort of treading water.

In short, Ortega's response to modernity is at the same time more realistic and more hopeful than any of the common Western responses reviewed above. It wisely avoids the excesses of both modernism and postmodernism and smartly trumps the distracted neoconservatives. Of course, Ortega's response is also far from being a complete strategy for overcoming modernity. It only begins to explain how humanity might come to stay afloat long enough to weather the crisis of modernity.

Pragmatism is another popular response to the crisis of modernity. Its champions, lead by philosophers Richard Rorty and John Dewey, have put forward a response that is in many respects very similar to Ortega's. Pragmatists argue that the answer to the problem of modern culture is to foster a "de-theoreticized sense of community" (Rorty 1985: 173) in which the practical concerns of social engineering will assert themselves over the philosophical bantering of modernists and postmodernists. "The way to re-enchant the world, to bring back what religion gave our forefathers, is to stick to the concrete" (Rorty 1985: 173). In *Philosophy and the Mirror of Nature* (1979), Rorty suggests that cultural values are/could be created by communities to meet their particular concrete needs. Truth and knowledge, as well as ethics and culture, are thus seen as free-floating, tied only to the needs and dialogue of the community.

This approach is similar to Ortega's in that it presents culture as dynamic and based on the immediate needs of the community, but it is very dissimilar from Ortega in at least two important respects. First, it fails to recognize the peril of the human condition in any way comparable to Ortega's view. In not seeing peril as the spur to cultural change, Rorty's pragmatism puts the community itself in charge of making those changes and so is vulnerable to charges that it could encourage the manipulation (and abuse) of culture (as postmodernists fear). Second, pragmatism does not escape the charge of hubris. In Ortega's philosophy, muddling through, or "treading water," will always be the best for which people can hope. Not so with pragmatism, which sees "social engineering" (Rorty 1985: 174) as the order of the day.

Clearly, Rorty has strong differences with Ortega (not to mention Bell) on the issue of human capabilities.[7]

Thus while Ortega shares many of his basic insights with pragmatists like Rorty and Dewey, there are also important differences between the two approaches. Despite a multitude of similarities, Ortega is neither modernist nor postmodernist, neither neoconservative nor pragmatist in his response to the problem of modernity. (See table 3.1 for a summary of these approaches.)

ORTEGA'S INFLUENCE ON SPANISH LITERATURE

Ortega's legacy for Latin America stems directly from the uniqueness of his response to the problems of modernity. His philosophy permeates the Spanish-speaking world and has heavily influenced succeeding generations of Latin American authors. At least four elements of Ortega's response to modernity could be described as deeply embedded in the Latin American literary tradition. These four elements will be referred to as personal scope, immediacy, continual struggle, and dignity in life.

"Personal scope" refers to Ortega's way of defining the struggle against modern cultural malaise as centered around individual choices about a life's project and personal dedication to that project. Unlike common European responses to modernity, Ortega does not see modernity as an anti-cultural leviathan that is too large for any one individual to overcome. Instead, the battle against modernity is fought in a thousand different ways by millions of very different individuals throughout modern society. Some fail to keep themselves above the waves, but others go on in the struggle using whatever stroke seems to work best for them. Each struggle is a different story, only collectively do they add up to society's crusade against the nihilism brought on by modernity. Most importantly, by this way of thinking the responsibility for maintaining the struggle does not rest with society, government, the family, or any other kind of distant group or association but with the individual himself, who must always strive to make the best of his shipwrecked condition.

"Immediacy" describes Ortega's setting for the struggle against modernity: life-threatening catastrophe. In contrast to other European responses to modernity, which invariably emphasize the very abstract philosophical nature of the problem of modernity, Ortega's response

Typical Responses	Content	Problematic Aspects	Self
Modernism	Retains faith in reason and order. Challenges old ways, constantly substituting new forms. Rapid change, constant innovation.	Subjectivity is latent at first, then leads to disorientation, fatigue and exhaustion. Ethics become problematic.	Strong in early stages; weak, isolated, and submissive in more developed forms.
Post-modernism	No faith in reason or order. All truth is contextual and power-oriented. "Deconstruction" is primary goal.	Cannot support renewed moral or ethical order. Abandons culture to embrace nihilism.	Weak and isolated, but not submissive.
Neo-conservatism	Rejects reason, but embraces traditional order. Man's "hubris" is the problem. Favors return to religion; or "a new revelation."	In seeking "deus ex machina," there is a failure to address the problem in human terms. Issue avoidance.	Weak and submissive, but not isolated.
Pragmatism	Seeks a "de-theoreticized sense of community." Order is created through the practical concerns of social engineering, not reason or philosophy.	"Social engineering" open to charges of manipulation. Culture may easily become based on power relationships. "Hubris" is a problem.	Strong, not isolated or submissive; too strong. Doesn't acknowledge human weakness. Subject to abuse of power.
Ortega's Response	Individual responsibility to struggle for continual renewal of human culture. Culture seen as kind of balanced outcome of rationalism and relativism.	Struggle has no easy answers or even (necessarily) any final hope, but problems of power and hubris are kept in their proper perspectives.	Strong, semi-isolated, semi-submissive. Admits weaknesses, but survival is possible.

Table 3.1 Summary of the typical responses to the crisis of modernity, including Ortega y Gasset's approach.

demands immediate and unequivocal decisions from individuals. They must constantly decide how to swim, or simply let themselves drown. Certainly Ortega's understanding of the problem is no less complex than the Germans', but his linking of the nature of the problem to the concerns of everyday life is much more successful because he brings the problem home to individuals. Failure to do anything has immediate and direct consequences for each person's own struggle to maintain a secure cultural and ethical foundation in his or her own life.

Even more important than these first two characteristics of Ortega's response to modernity is his understanding of the struggle against modernity as only an episode in humanity's "continual struggle" against the perils of existence. In effect, this observation changes the entire nature of the problem. Instead of being the kind of "end-of-history" threat that is commonly presented in German thought,[8] modernity loses its eschatological character and becomes a normal—even essential—part of the human experience. Though modernity retains its "crisis" atmosphere, the "task of our time" is no longer so hopeless as the "iron cage" image suggests. It may not ever be possible fully to escape the cage of modern culture, Ortega seems to be saying, but there may be ways of working around or expanding the limits it sets. Perhaps the cage itself is not so confining as it first appeared or perhaps it is really a cage no more limiting than our own bodies and brains or the great globe itself, as Shakespeare might have it. Perhaps still it is the same cage humans have always been living in, seen from the changed perspective of a new age. In any case, the important insight is that the crisis of modernity is not the final word on human values and culture. It doesn't even need to be the depressing fact of life it was for Weber. Muddling through modernity is simply "the task of our time" just as past ages had to muddle through their own problems and future ages will have new crises to face.

The fourth element of Ortega's thought that is deeply embedded in Latin American literature is its ability to see simple "dignity in life" as the solution not only to the problem of modernity but to all the historical crises that have beset humanity in the past and will continue to do so in the future. This goal of dignified living is in sharp contrast to typical European responses to modernity because it does not call for any kind of overcoming of the current situation or any escape from it. Instead of rejecting the modern condition as philosophically untenable, Ortega accepts it as the environment from which any effort to pursue a successful life must begin. Thus the goal of Ortega's philosophy is not really to overcome modernity at all, but rather to live successfully within its parameters.

All of these characteristics of Ortega's philosophy are distinctly "Latin" because they do not exist in other responses to the problem of modernity and because they have been repeatedly reflected in the work of Latin American authors since they appeared in the work of José Ortega y Gasset. The remainder of this study will show how Ortega's ideas about modernity participate in modern Latin American literature, and specifically, how they have influenced the works of three of Latin America's most prominent literary figures: Octavio Paz, Gabriel García Márquez, and Mario Vargas Llosa.[9]   It will also discuss how the understanding of modernity presented by these authors can suggest new strategies for living successfully within the confines of modern culture.

---

1. (Ortega y Gasset, 1956: 126). *"La vida es en sí misma y siempre un naufragio. Naufragar no es ahogarse. El pobre humano, sintiendo que se sumerge en el abismo, agita los brazos para mantenerse a flote. Esa agitación de los brazos con que reacciona ante su propia perdición, es la cultura--un movimiento natatorio. Cuando la cultura no es más que eso, cumple su sentido y el humano asciende sobre su propio abismo."*

2. A position strongly reminiscent of Max Weber's "Science as a Vocation" (See Weber, 1946: 155-156). Although he had specific disagreements with Weber on certain key sociological concepts, such as "social action" (see Pellicani: 116), it seems clear that Ortega agreed with many of Weber's ideas about modernity.

3. While it is true that a variety of distinct and competing theories certainly exists underneath the rubric of each of these types, they nevertheless may be thought of as "classes" of responses in the sense that specific theories within each group all share important characteristics particularly with regard to the issue of modernity.

4. Some would even characterize "postmodernism" as merely a kind of modernism or one aspect of modernism blown-up to its extreme form. Scaff, for example, regards postmodernism as "really aesthetic modernity with a prefixed afterthought" (Scaff: 235).

5. Note how similar this version of the decline of Western culture is to the one presented by Ortega in "The Revolt of the Masses" (Ortega y Gasset, 1932).

6. Note that this account is essentially similar to the commonly accepted version of "modernity as a cultural problem" discussed earlier(pp.19-23).

7. See Bell (1976) for a forceful critique of this view of human abilities.

8. Nietzsche, Marx, Weber, Simmel, Horkheimer & Adorno, and certainly Habermas all have this element present in their assessments of modern culture to varying degrees.

9. José Quiroga includes an interesting discussion of Ortega y Gasset's influence on Octavio Paz, for example (Quiroga: 61).

CHAPTER 4

The Life and Literature of Underdevelopment

> There is... another idea of art, or another idea of
> politics. Art here is neither subservient to the
> theoretical nor itself a kind of criticism of life...
> Instead there is a confusion of realms, a
> confusion of art and politics. They are the same
> activity... Politics, work, all human culture is
> symbol formation, is poetry.
>
> Jay Cantor (1981: 11)
> *The Space Between*

If politics and literature are understood to be complimentary activities, each dealing in and defined by the same symbolic currency, then literature is not only a reflection or expression of the social world but an integral part of the constant making and remaking of the political world itself. Art and politics become essentially the same activity, only expressed toward different ends and in a variety of differently proportioned 'symbolic solutions' mixed to create a desired reaction.[1]

An appropriate theoretical framework for understanding the relationship between politics and literature is provided by Karl Marx. According to Marx's *"homo faber"* [man the maker] thesis, "man's needs are historical, not naturalistic..." and human "activity is dynamic not only in relation to the object but in relation to the subject as well" (Avineri: 73, 75). That is, man's **labor** (as Marx would have it) changes both the environment and, subsequently, man himself, leading to new needs, desires, etc., and thus new forms of *labor* in a never ending dynamic cycle that constantly changes man and his world. Although Marx's thesis was intended to apply only to the material influences of the labor process, it is also used (often by other "marxist" theorists[2]) to explain relationships between people and ideas in human society. In this way an idealist application of the *homo faber* thesis is created, which is especially useful for understanding the relationship between literature and politics on the subject of modernity.[3] A *"homo saber"* [man the meaning-maker] thesis relating to the politics of culture would go something like this: Man's practice of **politics and art** (as the equivalent of "labor" in terms of symbol creation and manipulation), uses and subtly changes both the symbolic environment and, subsequently, man's own consciousness of himself, which leads to the practice of new forms of politics and art in a never ending dynamic cycle that constantly remakes man and his culture.

Modernity is a problem defined in terms of the weakening of cultural symbols and the loss of cultural meanings. It follows that the best way to understand this problem is in terms of its characteristic activities: politics and art. The political route to knowing modernity has already been pursued by many European social theorists, but in Latin America the more successful (and characteristic) form of analysis has been through the use of literature. If literature can provide insights into living with modernity that the science and reason routinely employed by European social thinkers has not been able to provide, then the result will surely be an improved understanding of the modern condition in both Europe and America.

Literature can teach a great deal about modern life because it provides a window into the consciousness of society that is not available elsewhere. Since modernity is a question that directly concerns social consciousness, literature could be the best way to explore the Latin American confrontation with modernity. More to the point, literature may itself be a most appropriate response to modernity. In many ways, literature is culture. It is one of the most direct ways for the "poor spent swimmer" to come to terms with his situation—to express the "movement of the arms" that is required to stay afloat (Ortega y Gasset, 1956: 126). It is one of the swimming strokes that Ortega hopes will carry the best of humanity's qualities forward to a time when the flood waters of modernity recede and new challenges rise to become the chief concern of future generations of shipwrecked human beings.

There is little question that literature is an important vehicle for political expression in Latin America, but why it is important is a matter of dispute. One common explanation for the phenomenon is that the authoritarian governments characteristic of the region make direct political critique dangerous. By this way of thinking, fiction provides a kind of shield for social critics. A competing explanation is that social critique through literature achieves a wider dissemination among the popular sectors of Latin America, giving the critic's ideas a greater impact on society than a straight academic discussion would. Although both of these ideas are no doubt correct to some degree, the best explanation in the light of Ortega's philosophy has to be that literature participates directly in the culture of Latin America in a way that strictly academic social critique does not.

Literature is a tool for social reform that is active both within and above culture, speaking the same symbolic language as culture, and in a real way defining culture at the same time that it challenges culture. Academic social critique, in contrast, is based on rationality—a language directly opposed to the duplicitous precision and parochialism of cultural symbols—and therefore outside of the Ortegan struggle to overcome catastrophe. After all, it is not science that Ortega sees as the force exerted to keep the poor spent swimmer afloat, but culture. What is at issue are the difficulties involved in achieving a way of life (or style of living, *"lebensführung"*)[4] conducive to human happiness within the given conditions of life. Literature is both a reaction to the suffering presented by an unsatisfying lifestyle and a radical attempt to redefine the conditions that gave rise to the suffering in the first place.

Is it any wonder then that "suffering" cultures produce great literature? That the modernization process itself creates conditions conducive to the writing of great literature is undeniable. Many of the greatest authors of the nineteenth century wrote on themes directly related to questions associated with modernization and the social changes that came with it. Indeed, there appears to be an especially important relationship between great literature and the experience of underdevelopment.

LIVING WITH UNDERDEVELOPMENT

The experience of underdevelopment occurs in cultures where economic modernity is forcefully imposed from above while the accompanying impetus toward social modernity, with its insistence on achieving real social and political equalities, is paradoxically opposed by the same forces.   Nowhere is this weird half-development better symbolized than in the stories of St. Petersburg, Russia and Brasília, Brazil.   Together they provide a telling account of the problems associated with living with underdevelopment.

St. Petersburg began as a swamp at the mouth of the Neva (or "mud") river, where Peter the Great envisioned a mighty city and naval base that would open Russia to modern Europe. It was built literally from nothing, achieving a population of close to 100,000 in only two decades (Berman: 177).   Designed entirely by foreign (European) architects and engineers, the city was laid out in a modern rectilinear pattern that was standard in the countries of Western Europe, but unknown in Russia. It was to be Peter's (and Russia's) great "window to Europe" and all the modern influences emanating from that region of the world.   Indeed, St. Petersburg was built to replace and deny medieval Moscow, with all its "centuries of tradition and... religious aura," as both the capitol of Russia and the symbolic core of the nation (Berman: 176-177).

Not everything about St. Petersburg was modern, however.   In many ways, the construction of the city proceeded by methods inconceivable in the West:

> Peter commanded every stonemason in the whole Russian Empire to relocate to the new construction site, and forbade building in stone anywhere else. He ordered a large proportion of noblemen not only to move to the new capital but to build palaces there, or forfeit their titles. Finally, in a serf society where the vast majority of people were property either of noble landowners or of the state, Peter had total power over a virtually infinite labor force. He forced these captives to work breathlessly to cut through the growth, drain the swamps, dredge the river, dig canals, raise and build the city at breakneck speed... In his will and his power to destroy his subjects en masse for the sake of construction, Peter was closer to the Oriental despots of ancient times—the Pharaohs with their pyramids, for instance—than to his fellow absolute monarchs in the West. (Berman: 177-178)

The result was a city rich in folklore and rich in contradictions between its modern ambitions and the medieval practices that continued to bind it to the past. In short, St. Petersburg became an archetypal setting for living "the modernism of underdevelopment."[5]

Brasília is in many ways a Latin American version of St. Petersburg. Like St. Petersburg, it was built from nothing (in this case the jungle of central Brazil) for the expressed purpose of becoming one of the most modern cities in the world. Like Petersburg, its construction was a massive undertaking made possible only though the full mobilization and centralized administration of state power. Like Petersburg, it was designed to be not only the new seat of political authority but also the foundation for an entirely new self-understanding in Brazil. As the Moscow-Petersburg axis represented the heart-brain struggle in Russia, so too would the contest between Brasília and the old coastal cities of nineteenth century Brazil.

Brasília is a city that was specifically designed to transform Brazilian society. It's founders sought both to create radically new social practices and to eliminate or deny older values. The ultimate goal of its designers was to "propel the country as a whole into the planned future it embodies" (Holston: 4, 79). The city is organized in the shape of a cross, with two wide transportation corridors: the North-South or 'Residential-Highway Axis' and the East-West or 'Monumental Axis'. Public buildings line the Monumental Axis, with the national executive, legislative, and judicial buildings at the East end in the "Square of the Three Powers," and municipal buildings on the West terminus. Great residential "*superquadras*" ("superblocks" or large apartment developments) fill the East and West wings of the city along the Residential-Highway Axis. It was originally hoped that the leveling effect of the *superquadras* would minimize class and status differences in Brasília, and lead to a whole new level of economic development across the country. Capitalist values of profit and property were to be minimized through the creative influence of architectural design (Holston: 76). It is precisely on this point (the perceived value of architectural style for bringing about social transformation) that the resemblance to St. Petersburg is most unmistakable.

Even the affectations of each city are similar, beginning with the methodical and ubiquitous presence of geometric patterns and extending to the apathy shown toward less prominent aspects of life in the city. In Petersburg, "the use of space behind the building facades was completely unregulated, so that, especially as the city grew, imposing exteriors could conceal festering slums" (Berman: 179). Brasília is itself a similar kind of facade, as the numerous *favelas*, or squatters' settlements (officially known as "satellite towns") that ring the central district make clear. These settlements are not allowed to take root in the city itself, in order to preserve the aesthetic unity of Brasília's design. "Thus it is possible to admire the science-fiction architectural marvels of the new capital, its miles and miles of soaring steel-and-glass edifices, and its heroic monuments, without being disturbed by the sights and smells of the poor" (Berger: 117).

There is one other important quality that these two cities share: Brasília has acquired Petersburg's reputation as "a strange, weird, spectral place," full of paradox and contradiction. Like St. Petersburg it practices "a politics of enforced backwardness in the midst of forms and symbols of enforced modernization" (Berman: 192-193).[6]   In Brasília, the most important contradiction is between the utopian vision of a fully modern city and the anti-utopian methods used to promote that vision:

> Founded on a paradox, Brasiliense society developed from the interaction of its utopic and dystopic elements. This dialectic generated new administrative initiatives as planners tried to keep the actual in line with the imagined. These directives, however, only reiterated the initial paradox: for planners responded to the deformation of their plans by exorcising the factors they held responsible (such as illegal squatter settlements, chaotic growth, and subversive political organization) by the same dystopic measures (such as denying political rights, repressing voluntary associations, and restricting the distribution of public goods).   Thus, in compounding the basic contradictions of Brasília's premises, they created an exaggerated version—almost a caricature—of what they had sought to escape. Their initiatives produced a unique city, but not the one they imagined. Rather, they turned Brasília into an exemplar of social and spatial stratification—one that clearly demonstrates, moreover, the role of government in promoting inequality. (Holston: 200)

Nineteenth-century St. Petersburg and twentieth-century Brasília are both spectral, ghostly towns because they seek to render invisible the common men and women who live and work behind their futuristic facades. The spirits walk their streets because for the first time in the history of their respective nations, the men and women of the great anonymous urban mass are no longer willing to remain undefined and unheard. The paradox of seeking to impose a facade of modernization from above and at the same time opposing the gathering momentum for social modernization from below is exactly what creates the most acute suffering of the human spirit in underdeveloped societies.

A powerful tension is created when social forces are arrayed in this way. When the common people begin to be ready to take possession of their public space but do not yet have the strength to overcome the powers of oppression, the result is a unique underground culture where those who are forbidden to live openly in the city streets and plazas live vigorously in the surreal half-light of "ill-lit lonely rooms" (Berman: 183). Sometimes, when the underground man surfaces to openly confront the powers, this shadow world erupts into the daylight world of city streets and police officers, but more often the struggle remains spectral, still political but experienced in the realm of culture and expressed through literature.

In St. Petersburg, the first open clash between "underground men" seeking the benefits of political modernity and the political authorities of the time occurred on December 14, 1825. The "Decembrist" revolt, as it came to be known, was a demonstration held in the Senate Square of St. Petersburg to protest the ascension of Tsar Nicholas I and promote constitutional reform. It was quickly and forcibly suppressed, but its importance for the underground culture of Petersburg cannot be overemphasized:

> If we see the city itself as a symbolic expression of modernization from above, December 14 represents the first attempt to assert, at the city's spatial and political center, an alternate mode of modernization from below. Till then, every definition and initiative in St. Petersburg emanated from the government; then suddenly the people—at least a segment of the people—were taking initiative into their own hands, defining Petersburg public space and its political life in their own way. (Berman: 181)

What followed this event was the full blossoming of Petersburg's brilliant literary tradition, "a tradition that focused obsessively on their city as a symbol of warped and weird modernity, and that struggled to take possession of this city imaginatively on behalf of the peculiar sort of modern men and women that Petersburg had made" (Berman: 181). For the next century, the tradition of writing literature as "a political as well as an artistic act" would be carried on by such celebrated figures as Alexander Pushkin, Nickolai Gogal, Feodor Dostoevsky, Leo Tolstoy,

Sergi Eisenstein, Andrei Biely, Evgeny Zamyatin, and Osip Mandelstam.[7]

The literary reaction to the conditions of modernity in Latin America followed this same pattern of development. Although Brasília experienced no revolt equivalent to Petersburg's Decembrist rebellion, the region as a whole suffered through many such clashes between the common people and the powers that be. To list all of Latin America's popular uprisings would be time consuming and unnecessary.[8] The important thing to note here is that many were similar to the Decembrist revolt in that they were carried out by "underground men" seeking to challenge the false modernity being imposed on them from above and begin the process of democratic modernization from below.[9]

It is possible to argue that the Latin American uprisings of the twentieth century, even when unsuccessful, marked the beginning of the great "boom" in Latin American literature in the same way that the Decembrist rebellion marked the beginning of St. Petersburg's classic literary tradition. Even more importantly, both literary movements can be understood to be cultural forces deployed to assist their respective peoples in a very political war: the war to break out of the modernism of underdevelopment and achieve a full modernity for all the inhabitants of St. Petersburg and Latin America.

THE LITERATURE OF UNDERDEVELOPMENT

The literature of underdevelopment is not without form. It is literature that seeks to challenge people's perceptions of their day to day experiences as they commute between the ubiquitous facades of modernization and the depressing reality of social backwardness. Three aspects of life are especially important targets: natural physical reality; the isolated self, and absolutist orthodoxies.   These "targets" for criticism may be thought of as the literature of underdevelopment's 'critique of natural reality', 'critique of culture', and 'critique of power'. Through these critiques, both nineteenth century Russian and contemporary Latin American literature challenge people's perceptions of the physical, cultural, and political realities of their existence. The unwritten purpose of the critiques is immanent within the very experience of their being; it is to make the invisible man see himself and, at least partially, claim his right to political existence in the modern world. Of course, simply seeing oneself in the light of the surrounding struggle is not to triumph in any ultimate way, but it is to keep from drowning in the nothingness of enforced modernity; it is, as Ortega would have it, to continue to exist in a responsible, meaningful way.

The critique of natural reality uses unstable, contradictory, or otherwise questionable depictions of physical reality to cast doubt on the modern 'scientific' understanding of reality as something objective and separate from the observing individual. By undercutting the authority of these truth claims, the critique opens up a space for deliberation about the ethics of 'progress' and the relentless pursuit of the new that is so much a part of the lifestyle of modernity.

The critique of culture focuses on the isolation of the self in modern society. Solitude is depicted as the central feature of existence in the modern milieu, and escape from the disconnected self is a recurring (though sometimes latent or unrecognized) heroic theme. This critique of the self in modernity has the effect of focusing attention on modernity's most antihuman implications and pushing readers to explore new ways to achieve fulfillment through interpersonal connectedness.

The critique of power exists to explode the authority of absolutism and orthodoxy. The enforcement of the "modernism of underdevelopment" is the clear target of this critique, and its neglect of the public sphere is the chief wrong that the critique seeks to set right. By attacking the evil inherent in authoritarian modes of development, the critique provokes a search for ways to make the deliberative ideals of the Enlightenment a reality in modernity.

Latin America's contribution to the literature of underdevelopment is best understood by exploring these three critiques within the context of its modern literary masterpieces. Certainly, the region is no stranger to political literature. Almost every historical period and philosophical movement prominent in Latin America has been represented by at least one fictional narrative expression.[10] In Mexico, José Joaquín Fernández de Lizardi (1776-1827) supported the liberal cause of independence in several novels, including his famous *El Periquillo Sarniento (The Itching Parrot)* and *Conversations of the Peasant and the Sacristan.*[11]

In the age of Argentine independence, poet Esteban Echeverría (1805-1851) and statesman Domingo Faustino Sarmiento (1811-1888), author of *Facundo, o civilización y barbarie en las pampas argentinas* (or simply *Facundo*, as it is more commonly known)[12] contributed their literary talents. Among the many literary figures associated with the philosophy of positivism in Latin America are Ecuador's Juan Montalvo

(1832-1889), Cuban hero and poet José Martí (1853-1895), Peruvian Manuel González Prada (1848-1918), and Brazilian Euclydes da Cunha (1868-1909).[13]   José Enriqué Rodó (1872-1917) used Shakespeare's figure of *Ariel* in his book of the same name to promote a uniquely Latin American blend of liberalism and traditionalism, positivism and idealism, and democracy and aristocracy that has since become a classic in Latin American political thought.

Many of these works are rich in themes relating to the modernism of underdevelopment, but the contributions of contemporary Latin American authors possess a maturity in their portrayal of modernity that the older literature simply can not match. Of the present-day authors whose work is known for its powerful critique of modern life, three of the region's most widely recognized literary figures stand out in particular: Octavio Paz of Mexico, Gabriel García Márquez of Colombia, and Mario Vargas Llosa of Peru.

Octavio Paz is known primarily as a poet, but he is also justifiably famous for his numerous essays on social concerns in Mexico and Latin America. His works present a rare mix of both cultural/literary insights and political/philosophical commentary. Jurgen Habermas has cited Paz in connection with his own work on the pathologies of modernity, and it is clear from reading Paz that he is directly concerned with the problem of modernity in the Latin American context.[14]   Paz's response to modernity, in particular his emphasis on the role of criticism in the modern context and his portrayal of Zapatism as a way around modern fragmentation, is one of the greatest Latin American contributions to the philosophical discourse of modernity (and closely parallels José Ortega y Gasset's main themes). Among Paz's more prominent works related to the theme of Modernity are *The Labyrinth of Solitude*, *The Other Mexico*, and *Conjunction and Disjunctions*.

Gabriel García Márquez is presently Latin America's most renown novelist and has repeatedly addressed topics relevant to the concerns of modern social critics and political theorists in his literary work. Many of his novels (particularly his Nobel-prize winning *One Hundred Years of Solitude*) present a picture of modern man that is difficult to ignore. His poetic depiction of the solitude associated with the modern individual's confrontation with an unknowably complex and fragmented world fits well with European images of modernity. Additionally, his use of what has been called "magic realism" (depicting normal events as if they were wonders and impossible events as if they were commonplace) carries unmistakable signs of the modernism of underdevelopment. Reality, García Márquez seems to say, can include our dreams about politics and community as well as the way we live these things in everyday life.

Finally, Mario Vargas Llosa has been personally active in politics for some time. His literary accomplishments are rich in insight about the Latin American experience of modernity. Novels such as *The Time of the Hero*, *The Green House*, and *Conversation in the Cathedral* became famous for the way they portray reality in fragmented and confused but ultimately multifaceted ways. Truth in the novel is indistinct for Vargas Llosa in much the same way as it is for Paz, García Márquez and other modern authors. His literary technique relies on such devices as "telescopic conversations," diverse "planes of reality" and seemingly random leaps in time—all leading to a depiction of the world as complicated, imposing, immoral and strangely unrevealed. In his later works (such as *The War of the End of the World*, and *The Real Life of Alejandro Mayta*) there is less of this kind of literary fragmentation, but more of the direct political commentary that eventually lead him to be an active writer about real-world politics. In any case, the depiction of Latin American life throughout Vargas Llosa's works is constant. An infernal atmosphere pervades most of his writing, poisoning any possibility for heroism, self-honesty or genuine love. As with the real-world countries of Latin America, progress with a human face seems impossible amid the onslaught of modern pressures.

The three critiques characteristic of the literature of underdevelopment are all aggressively pursued by each of these three great Latin American authors, though each author has his own particular way of presenting them. The chapters that follow are organized thematically to explore the different ways that the critiques are manifested in the work of Paz, García Márquez and Vargas Llosa. Chapter five, entitled "Time and Reality," explores themes related to the critique of natural reality. Chapter six, "Solitude and Love," brings together the various authors' consideration of ideas reflecting the critique of culture. Chapter seven, "Power, Politics, and Recovery," considers the critique of power and each author's response to the problem of power in the context of underdevelopment.

1. The relationship between politics and cultural symbols has been established in many different studies, but the work of Murray Edelman (1967 & 1988, for example) remains the classic consideration of this subject.

2. Most notably Italian Marxist Antonio Gramsci (1985), for example, but also Max Horkheimer (1972), Theodore Adorno (1983), Herbert Marcuse (1964), Louis Althusser (1996), and many others.

3. Though Marx would hardly have agreed with this application, since it displaces his emphasis on "productive labor" as the means for transforming the world (see Avineri: 65-95 for more on the *Homo Faber* thesis).

4. The term is Max Weber's (among others). See Hennis (1987: 62-104) for more on this idea.

5. The term is Marshall Berman's (Berman: Chapter IV, "Petersburg: The Modernism of Underdevelopment").

6. The words are from Berman's description of St. Petersburg; they are equally valid for Brasilia.

7. For a zesty discussion of the most well-known works of these figures, see Berman's (173-248) chapter on the modernism of underdevelopment.

8. Some of the most important include the Mexican Revolution (1910-1920), resistance to the dictatorship of Gertulio Vargas in Brazil (1950s), the Cuban Revolution (1969), the Nicaraguan Revolution (1979), resistance to the rule of Augusto Pinochet in Chile (1980s), and the current "Zapatísta" rebellion in the Mexican state of Chiapas. Numerous other uprisings have occurred throughout the last half-century in Colombia, Venezuela, El Salvador, and Peru (to name a few).

9. There has been much discussion in the United States concerning the extent to which many of these rebellions have been instigated by Cuba or communist states outside of the Western Hemisphere. The issue remains largely unresolved, but there can be little doubt that many of Latin America's uprisings were in fact homegrown expressions of popular displeasure with dictatorial and oppressive regimes.

10. Brief reviews of the achievements of all of the following authors may be found in W. Rex Crawford's *A Century of Latin American Thought* (1963) and Harold Eugene Davis' *Latin American Thought: A Historical Introduction* (1972).

11. Originally published in Mexico as *Conversaciones del payo y el sacristán* (1824). English excerpts are available in Harold Eugene Davis' *Latin American Social Thought* (1961).

12. Translated in English as *Facundo: Life in the Argentine Republic in the Days of the Tyrants, or, Civilization and Barbarism* (1972).

13. Euclydes da Cunha's account of the strange revolt at Canudos in the Backlands of Brazil (*Os sertões: Campanha de Canudos*, translated by Samuel

Putnam as *Rebellion in the Backlands*) is neither purely literature nor exactly history. Nevertheless, it would later provide the basis for Mario Vargas Llosa's masterful *The War of the End of the World*, which is considered in detail throughout subsequent sections of this study.

14. Habermas cites Paz in *The Philosophical Discourse of Modernity*: "Only when the subject *loses* itself, when it sheers off from pragmatic experience in space and time, when it is stirred by the shock of the sudden, when it considers 'the longing for true presence' (Octavio Paz) fulfilled and, oblivious to itself, is transported by the moment..." (Habermas: 93).

CHAPTER 5

Time and Reality

> The reality to which we give the name of
> civilization does not allow of easy definition. It
> is each society's vision of the world and also its
> feeling about time.[1]

Octavio Paz (1985: 358-359)
Mexico and the United States

The critique of natural reality presented in much of Latin American literature challenges the Western understanding of reality as something objective and separate from the observing individual.   This kind of critique is, of course, not new in the philosophical discourse of modernity.   Modern people's fragmented experience of time is closely related to the characteristic transformations of modernity identified by Western scholars and critics.[2]   The theme of broken reality is also not unique to the Latin American context.   It recalls much of what was characterized earlier as the philosophical and cultural problems of modernity.

Nevertheless, the fact that Latin American authors frequently use these themes highlights their concern with the problems of modernity. Moreover, the unique ways that they have of presenting the Latin American experience of time and reality reveals much about their understanding of the modernism of underdevelopment.   Octavio Paz, Mario Vargas Llosa, and Gabriel García Márquez each address the themes of time and reality in their work. Collectively, their ideas present a broad canvass from which a general appreciation of Latin America's approach to time and reality can be discerned. In the end, these authors' presentation of time and reality shows that their appreciation of the problem of modernity is very similar to that of European thinkers and also uncovers the region's indebtedness to the ideas of José Ortega y Gasset.

TIME

Octavio Paz divides time into two main categories or types: "chronometric time" and "mythological time." This division sets up an opposition through which much Latin American literature can be interpreted. It is an opposition that Paz attributes, indirectly, to José Ortega y Gasset (Paz 1985: 212). In fact, many of the Spanish philosopher's ideas can be found by analyzing how "time" is presented in modern Latin American literature.

"Chronometric time" is, according to Paz, "a homogeneous succession lacking all particularity. It is always the same, always indifferent to pleasure or pain" (Paz 1985: 209). Chronometric time is, of course, associated with modern, developed states and with the lifestyle of modern individuals who measure their lives in minutes and hours, months and years. This is normally not a very difficult concept for people to grasp. Mythological time (or "original time" as Paz also refers to it), on the other hand, is more challenging:

> Mythological time... is impregnated with all the particulars of our lives: it is as long as eternity or as short as a breath, ominous or propitious, fecund or sterile. This idea allows for the existence of a number of varying times. Life and time coalesce to form a single whole, an indivisible unity. (Paz 1985: 209)

The contrast is meant to highlight not merely two different ways of understanding time, but two completely different modes of living. The difference is between the normal, everyday experience of living in a sequential flow of time from moment to moment, and living in a perpetual present that Paz associates with a kind of universal transcendence:

> There was a time when time was not succession and transition, but
> rather the perpetual source of a fixed present in which all times, past
> and future, were contained. (Paz 1985: 209)

In universal transcendence, man's "subjective life becomes identical with
exterior time, because this has ceased to be a spatial measurement and
has changed into a source, a spring, in the absolute present, endlessly
re-creating itself" (Paz 1985: 211).   Moreover, original time also
transcends the individual's isolation in modernity, and "opens the doors
of communion" (Paz 1985: 211).

According to Paz, everyone starts life in the absolute present of
original time, but individuals lose it or are "expelled" from it upon
becoming aware of other 'presents', as well as the past and the future:

> My time—the time of the garden, the fig tree, the games with
> friends, the drowsiness under the sun at three in the afternoon amid
> the grasses...—was a fictitious time. In spite of what my senses
> told me, the time from over there, that of the others, was the truth,
> the time of the real present. I accepted the inevitable: I was grown
> up [adult]. That was how my expulsion from the present began.
> (my translation)[3]

The   need   for   transcendence   arises   with   the   presence   of
chronometric time, which Paz has referred to as a "rationalization" of
the "flow of reality" (Paz 1985: 210).

> When man was exiled from that eternity in which all times were
> one, he entered chronometric time and became a prisoner of the
> clock and the calendar... Man ceased to be one with time, ceased to
> coincide with the flow of reality... These spatial measurements of
> time separate man from reality—which is a continuous present—
> and turn all the presences in which reality manifests itself... into
> phantasms. (Paz 1985: 209)

For Paz (and other Latin American writers), the crying need of
modernity is to reassert the presence of original time in the modern
world. Speaking of the contemporary crisis in rational modernity, Paz
asserts that "the present requires much more than attention to immediate
needs; it demands global soul-searching. For a long time I have firmly
believed that the twilight of the future heralds the advent of the now"
(Paz 1990: 30).

There are a variety of ways for individuals to experience original time, but the archetypal method (at least in Mexico) is through the religious ritual, or *fiesta*.

> A fiesta is something more than a date or anniversary. It does not celebrate, but *reproduces* an event: it opens [breaks, splits] in two chronometric time so that, for the space of some brief but immeasurable time period, the eternal present is reinstated. The fiesta becomes creator of time. Repetition becomes conception. Time is begotten. The golden age returns. (my translation)[4]

In this way the experience of original time is brought about through a 'return' to what Paz characterizes as "the absolute present" (Paz 1985: 211). The place of tradition in this return to the present is not an error: "modernity breathes life in to tradition, and tradition responds by providing depth and gravity" (Paz 1990: 20).

But ritual is not the only way of reawakening the absolute present. For Paz the theater, the poem, and the novel or story are all ways of reproducing events in such a way that chronometric time is destroyed and the eternal present reinstated. "Being a Mexican writer means listening to the voice of that present—that presence. Listening to it speaking with it, deciphering it, expressing it..." (Paz 1990: 10). In fact, not only Mexican but much of Latin American literature in general seeks to achieve this liberation from the chronometric time of modernity. It is an effort that Paz traces back to the thought of José Ortega y Gasset,[5] and it is also actively pursued by both Mario Vargas Llosa and Gabriel García Márquez.

Mario Vargas Llosa's first three major novels (*The Time of the Hero, The Green House*, and *Conversation in the Cathedral*)[6] are marked by an extraordinary attempt (largely successful) to use literary technique to master the way time is presented in the written story. His particular genius is the ability to force readers to experience a taste of what Paz might call "the absolute present." Speaking of *The Green House*, but in words that could be applied equally well to any of the three novels mentioned above, Vargas Llosa claims of his novel that "there is no linear order. I have tried to give all of the worlds—so opposite, so different—as a totality" (Vargas Llosa, quoted in Moody: 408). Key to Vargas Llosa's effort to capture a "total present" are the techniques of multiplicity, disjunction, simultaneity, and ambiguity.

These techniques are used most forcefully in Vargas Llosa's employment of what critics call "telescoped dialogues" (Williams 1986: 51).[7]

Telescoped dialogues appear toward the end of *The Time of the Hero*, are used frequently in *The Green House*, and achieve a bewildering effect in *Conversation in the Cathedral*. They involve multiple dialogues from different times and places being interpolated into one narrative conversation in such a way that the segments seem to fit with each other in tone and/or theme. Consider the following simple dialogue from *The Green House*:

> "But you already told me about that when we left the island, Fushía," Aquilino said. "I want to hear how you escaped."
>
> "With this picklock," Chango said. "Iricuo made it from a wire on his cot. We tried it out and it can open the door without any noise. You want to see, Jappy?" he said to Fushía.
>
> Chango was the older one, he was in for drugs or something, and he was good to Fushía. Iricuo, on the other hand, was always making fun of him. A slippery guy who had swindled a lot of people with a story about an inheritance. He was the one who made the plans.
>
> "And it happened just like that, Fushía?" Aquilino asked.
>
> "Just like that," Iricuo said... (Vargas Llosa 1968: 22)

The dialogue seems to fit together logically, but the conversation actually takes place on two different temporal levels. The Fushía-Aquilino dialogue takes place in the immediate present, while the Fushía-Chango-Iricuo dialogue happens in a kind of past present.

> This technique has two effects. On the one hand, the use of actual dialogue from the past—rather than a character's observation of it—makes the reader's experience with even the remote past direct... On the other hand, this technique of telescoping dialogues creates juxtapositions of an occasionally contradictory and paradoxical nature: the reader experiences a capricious reality that seems to be perpetually relative to circumstances and the subjectivity of the individual speaking. (Williams 1986: 52)

The end result is often "a kind of psychic leak in which emotions abound that may or may not be attached to any single character, thus lending the text or scene a sense or feeling as though it were a character itself" (Cheuse: 449). Or, as another critic has put it: "the use of these new techniques makes possible not only the expression of different levels of reality but also the exclusion of distance between reader and narrator, taking the former directly into the reality created by the book" (Moreno Turner: 27).

Consider the following telescoped dialogue from *Conversation in the Cathedral*:

> "He doesn't want to go to the Catholic University but to San Marcos," señora Zoila said. "That upset Fermín very much."
>
> "I'll bring him to his senses, Zoila, don't you get involved," Don Fermín said. "He's at the foolish age, you have to know how to lead him. If you fight with him, he'll get all the more stubborn."
>
> "If instead of advice you'd give him a couple of whacks, he'd pay more attention to you," Señora Zoila said. "The one who doesn't know how to raise him is you."
>
> "She married that boy who used to come to the house," Santiago says. "Popeye Arévalo, Freckle Face Arévalo."
>
> "Skinny doesn't get along with his old man because they don't have the same ideas," Popeye said.
>
> "And what ideas does that snotnose still wet behind the ears have?" The senator laughed.
>
> "Study hard, get your law degree and you can dip your spoon into politics," Don Fermín said. "Right Skinny?"
>
> "Skinny gets mad because his old man backed Odría in his revolt against Bustamante," Popeye said. "He's against the military." (Vargas Llosa 1975: 22-23)

There are six separate dialogues going on in this passage, each distinct not only in space but also in time.[8]   The result is that "the textual continuity and coherence is effected not by chronological sequencing, but rather by an intricate series of verbal and pragmatic clues, which allow a temporally disconnected set of discourse to be interpreted as textually connected" (Lipski: 73). By using this method, Vargas Llosa "does not violate the characters' independent viewpoints. Nor does he resort to the generalizing and poeticizing which some Latin American novelists have relied upon to establish distance between themselves and the narrative context" (Edwards: 23).

At one point in *Conversation in the Cathedral*, no fewer than eighteen separate dialogues are interlaced in a single conversation. The net result of all these conversations, together with other techniques for achieving the kind of displacement that Vargas Llosa is striving to achieve, is reminiscent of Paz's ideas concerning the absolute present:

> For the reader, all of the fragments seem to coexist within a framework where the point of reference is always the present... Vagueness in the treatment of time is a deliberate part of the author's method and quite essential to the novel's meaning. By dramatizing the content of the characters' memories as well as their present, he makes all of reality seem contemporaneous. Within each fragment of narrative, everything merges into simultaneity. Guided by this kind of portrayal, the reader experiences an immensely heightened sense of immediacy. (Moody: 425)

Thus Paz's absolute present is recreated in the literary style and technique of Mario Vargas Llosa.

But Paz's absolute present is of course more than simply the dominance of the present tense. Paz clearly also includes a kind of wholeness or completeness in his conception of the 'golden age.' This wholeness can also be found in Mario Vargas Llosa's rendition of the absolute present. *The Green House* is exemplary in this respect.

The Green House is built around five separate plot lines taking place in different locations (notably the town of Piura in Northern Peru and the Peruvian jungle), and each involving "not only a different time level but a different internal ordering of time" (Moody: 415).[9]

> As he progresses through the novel, the reader does not perceive the internal temporal design that underlies the arrangement of each narrative and that thus serves as a source of unity for the many dislocated fragments. Instead, he observes the concurrent advance of all the plots, which produces a continual overlapping of temporal levels so that characters and events are simultaneously viewed from various perspectives and at different distances in time. (Moody: 415)

The overall effect is one of what Gregory Rabassa, Vargas Llosa's translator for *The Green House*, has called "total time":

> Vargas Llosa has tried to present total time, the time of this whole period, where moments are only relative to each other, relative to the way in which they are seen together in what is deceptively the same time. It might be compared to what happens at night when we go out and look at the stars. We see all the stars together at the

same time. But we don't. The light from each star is arriving here at a different time. No two stars are that close together. Vargas Llosa brings all the times together to show their relevance to this moment, not to history. (Rabassa: 21)

Thus the fragmentation of time gives rise to a kind of wholeness in which all times are one. Divisional measurements cease to exist and all is, as Paz would have it, a timeless condition of the eternal present.

It is within this timelessness that the first traces of a cyclic (or traditional) wholeness can be discovered.

Events themselves, as they are portrayed in each story, strongly suggest that human existence in all its facets is cyclic and, in a sense, timeless. While structural fragmentation underscores the breakup of individual personality in a disordered world, certain elements within the stories establish temporal continuity on other levels. Something humanly permanent exits beneath the fleeting, disconnected moments experienced by the characters. Although disassociated from themselves and from their personal histories, the characters enact human dramas that are framed by either generic or symbolic reference and, therefore, belong to the cyclic flow of an endless past...

On the level of symbolism, the cyclic quality of time acquires its full meaning in yet another dimension... The appearance of archetypal patterns suggests that man must relive the same conflicts and imperfections that compose the unchanging realities of human experience. (Moody: 426-427)

The appearance of these archetypal patterns is what introduces the traditional element into Vargas Llosa's version of the absolute present and also what has lead some critics to point to "myth" as a constitutive element of his work.[10]

However one understands the wholeness that lies behind the fragmented pieces of time with which Vargas Llosa assembles *The Green House*, the net effect is to "reveal the timeless dimension of human tragedies" (Moody: 427). This is an equivalent to Octavio Paz's conception of the absolute present. It is also equivalent to Ortega y Gasset's existentialist vision of life as shipwreck. Life is seen to compel the characters of the Green House to participate in shaping their own destiny, but it also limits severely the possibilities available to them.

> For nearly all the characters, life represents an intolerable cycle of
> entrapment and escape that reduces their aspirations to thoughts of a
> sanctuary where, in the places of their origins, they might find some
> alleviation from the final experience of extinction. (Moody: 427)

That sanctuary in the place of their origin is in the communal experience
of Paz's original time. Their efforts to experience this sanctuary are the
swimming motion of Ortega y Gasset's poor shipwrecked human being.

The timeless wholeness that Vargas Llosa illuminates through his
method of fragmenting present moments of time into a kind of universal
collage is summoned in a more direct way by Gabriel García Márquez.
In such novels as *One Hundred Years of Solitude*, *The Autumn of the
Patriarch*, and *Chronicle of a Death Foretold*,[11]   García Márquez
presents time as cyclical and mythical, achieving the same kind of vision
of a timeless present where all the successes and failures of human life
are played out in an endless repetition of the human drama. At the same
time, linear time is portrayed in a struggle against the cyclical patterns of
life, leading individuals against the circular flow of time and into
modernity. Here again, one can appreciate the similarities between this
vision of the human condition and those of Octavio Paz and José Ortega
y Gasset.

One Hundred Years of Solitude is Gabriel García Márquez's most
famous novel. It traces the history of the Buendía family and at the
same time tells the story of their town, Macondo, from its original
founding to its ultimate obliteration in a hurricane. The movement from
origin to destruction is a sign of the mythical dimensions of García
Márquez's use of time, but the conditions prevailing at the time of the
founding of Macondo give readers a clear impression of the "absolute
present" of Paz's "original time":

> Macondo's establishment takes place in a primeval setting, and it
> represents the union of man with nature. Octavio Paz suggests that
> the myth of the golden age "*no está en la naturaleza ni en las
> historia sino entre ellas: en ese instante en que los hombres
> fundan su agrupación con un pacto que, simultáneamente, los une
> entre ellos y une al grupo con el mundo natural.*" García Márquez
> considers this vision more important than the discovery and
> conquest themes. Macondo, therefore, becomes a variant of the
> myth of the golden age, or paradise.[12] (Sims: 142)

Additionally, the format of the novel itself is conducive to giving readers an impression of the 'absolute present', for the novel is functionally equivalent to the family history that the gypsy Melquíades presents to José Arcadio Buendía within the story. In that family history, Melquíades wrote about the events in the novel as if they had all happened together at the same moment in time (García Márquez 1970: 382). The first sentence of the novel sets the tone by having a character look forward to a time in his life when he would be remembering the events about to be narrated (García Márquez 1970: 11).

Action in passages like these is not chronological. Instead, "it has the function of evoking the end of a vital cycle from its beginning, so that the present is seen from the perspective of the past, a projection the future will give it" (McNerney: 19-20). In effect, "throughout the novel the narration is in a closed time, with a beginning and an end; and all of whose 'times,' present, past, and future, can be recounted at any time by the narrator, who is equidistant from them all" (McNerney: 20). The end result for the reader is an odd feeling of uncertainty about time:

> García Márquez's manipulation of time and creation of a closed, all-encompassing system within the book forces the reader to doubt the usual linear conception and measurement of time, and in fact calls into question the very time of the book itself. For if Melquíades's parchments are a history of the family, they are also its prophecy; they predate the actions they describe. (McNerney: 20-21)

In this way, cyclical time and the absolute present subtly become one of the first things the reader encounters in *One Hundred Years of Solitude*.

The golden age of original time is also captured in the cyclicality of García Márquez's novels. The structure of *The Autumn of the Patriarch* presents a fine example:

> The novel's spiral structure conveys an impression of mythical time, i.e., a sense of endless renewal, tending to negate temporal progression, and thus escape from the terrors of history, into a realm of absolute stability. (McMurray 1977: 135)

Even *Chronicle of a Death Foretold* gives the impression of cycles of time, though here they are somewhat sinister in that the cycles help to cover up the specifics of a murder to which time seems an accomplice.

> The wisdom of "Time will tell" does not apply here. The opposite
> is true; time will reduce to silence. The narrator's efforts are to
> rescue an event from the leanness it has acquired in memory, as he
> tries to flesh out the details of a story that is starting to evaporate, to
> rot, with water invading the town archives, and with language and
> memory still circling like scavengers over a death that remains
> inexplicable, even if many times foretold and retold. (Pope: 186)

The murder of Santiago Nasser is "foretold" because the traditions of the
golden age of cyclical, original time demand it. It is a foregone
conclusion that he must die and the whole town expects it. His death is
a tragedy because he is innocent of any wrongdoing, but the cycles of
renewal characteristic of original time serve to wipe away the stain of
the murder (a more correct term for his departure) and the town soon
forgets the whole affair. As a final symbol of renewal, the rejected bride
(Angela Vicario) and her would-be husband (Beyardo San Román) are
eventually reconciled and reunited.

One Hundred Years of Solitude also successfully uses cyclical
patterns to achieve the effect of the continual renewal associated with
mythical and original time: "Although the novel is essentially
chronological, author and characters perceive life not as an episode
adventure-story along the lines of the "traditional novel," but as a
recurring design" (Foster: 36). In fact, the whole novel is contained
within a grand, overarching cycle based on the Buendía family's fear of
revisiting a family curse:

> The narrative is a tale with a tail on both ends. It begins with
> incestuous love resulting in the birth of a son with a pig's tail, and
> ends with incestuous love resulting in the birth of a son with a pig's
> tail. This rounds out the tale, which begins where it ends, and ends
> where it begins. The basic form of the novel, then, is a circle.
> (Watson: 90)

The Autumn of the Patriarch has a similar way of coming full circle, but
here the image is one of the impending end of time itself:

> In the closing of the circle, when the body is finally accepted as the
> general's and his death can be believed at last, it can be announced
> to the world that "the uncountable time of eternity had come to an
> end" (251). (McNerney: 60)

The repetition of cycles in these novels injects mythical (or original) time into the flow of events, offering "a temporary escape from the harsh realities of history by rendering the impression of an eternal present, constantly revitalized by recurring configurative patterns" (McMurray 1977: 76). The most obvious recurring pattern in *One Hundred Years of Solitude* is the repetition of names and traits across generations in the Buendía family. Not only do the names José Arcadio and Aureliano reappear with each new generation, but also their traits: the José Arcadios are invariably passionate and industrious while the Aurelianos are clearheaded but distant.

Similar kinds of repetitions are abundant and reinforce the circular structure of the novel and cyclical concept of time. Colonel Aureliano's interminal labor on his little gold fishes are a memorable example:

> It is not just that they get made and then melted down again over and over (content), but that the story of their getting made and melted down, and of other things getting built and torn down and built up again, keeps getting repeated over and over (form). (Watson: 90)

Similarly, Aureliano Segundo's destruction of the Buendía house's vases and mirrors during the time of great rain represents the end of one cycle and the beginning of a renewal for the family. ('Rain' is itself a symbol of cleansing and renewal here.) After methodically destroying everything in the house that was breakable he went out and returned before midnight with food. From then on the family did not go hungry (García Márquez 1970: 302).

A most amusing cycle that also reinforces the image of cyclical time is identified by critic Richard Watson:

> Here is a final epicycle. Colonel Aureliano dies standing under the chestnut tree with this head propped against the trunk. If his father's body is not buried under that tree, at least his ghost is still rotting there, so the circle goes from the ghost of Colonel Aureliano's father through the ground, into the tree, from the tree trunk into Colonel Aureliano's forehead down through his body to his feet to the ground again. What is more, the critical tool that opens and closes this story is hanging out, for Colonel Aureliano dies in the business of pissing on his father's ghost, which he has been doing over and over again for a very long time. There is a pig's tale for you. (Watson: 91)

Finally, the history of the family itself is the story of a cyclical rising and falling of family fortunes. Pilar Ternera understood that the history of the Buendías was like a machine that carried out ceaseless repetitious cycles. She also knew that the only thing that could stop the endless repetition in the family would be the inevitable and irremediable wear and tear on the machine itself (García Márquez 1970: 364). The Buendías would go on repeating the same patterns and cycles until they simply wore out from the repetition.

Needless to say, despite the presence of mythical time in García Márquez's novels, the 'harsh realities of history' are also present. In many ways, it is the individual's tendency to experience time as a linear progression rather than as a repeating cycle that leads to the tragedies of human existence. For it is only within the context of the linear experience of time that human tragedies are actually seen as tragic. When put into the context of mythical time, the troubles of individual characters become the timeless tragedies of human existence, lending them the same immortal quality that distinguished Vargas Llosa's eternal present.

For Macondo, the end of the innocence that characterized the golden age of original time is represented by the insomnia and forgetfulness plague of chapter three. Up to this time (and for a little while after) no one has yet died in the town of Macondo (García Márquez 1970: 61)—a symbol of the renewing effects of cyclical time. But the advent of reason would bring about the destruction of memory (tradition/ritual) and lead to a new conception of time:

> The destruction of memory, the efforts to retain human knowledge, and Melquíades's magic potion, convey metaphorically the emergence of Macondo from the status of an archaic, prehistoric community constantly revitalized by the principle of cosmogonic, cyclical renewal to a society characterized by its detachment from nature, its awareness of the historic past, and its acceptance of irreversible lineal time. (McMurray 1977: 75)

Similarly, the life of Úrsula Buendía may be interpreted as one long struggle against the ravages of linear time. She is repeatedly associated with cyclical events and constantly depicted as attempting to rejuvenate the life of the family.

An archetypal representation of the wise and energetic matriarch, Úrsula does her utmost to bolster family unity, ward off the curse of incest, and prevent injustice. Her quest for permanence and stability in a world increasingly menaced by chaos is underscored by her acute awareness of the cyclical nature of time. Thus, as she observes the irrational behavior reappearing in each generation of her descendants, her oft-repeated statement that time is not passing but turning in a circle does not necessarily convey despair but rather an illusion of a perpetual present. Her own actions also emphasize the principle of regeneration as exemplified by her repeated renovations of the Buendía home, the first time in order that Amaranta and Rebecca can entertain their young friends, again at the end of the civil wars, and finally after the rains have ceased. (McMurray 1977: 77-78)

Úrsula thus plays a role that García Márquez has often identified as characteristic of the women in his novels. "I think women keep the world going and stop everything falling apart while men try and push history forward" (Mendoza and García Márquez: 76).

Úrsula is the longest-lived character in *One Hundred Years of Solitude* and her longevity is surely attributable to her many connections with cyclical time. Nevertheless, as linear time becomes dominant in Macondo, even Úrsula cannot resist its destructive consequences.

As the years pass, Úrsula begins to sense "everyday reality slipping through her hands" and gradually comes to realize that "the progressive disruption of time" is her worst enemy. In spite of her astonishing will to survive, her frustrations due to blindness and old age make her increasingly aware of the lack of meaning in her existence. Her situation reaches the height of the absurd during the rains when, shrunken and failing mentally, she becomes a toy for her mischievous great-great-great-great- grandson Aureliano Babilonia... After the rains she makes a brief but valiant effort to restore order to the household, but she soon loses contact with reality, begins to live in the distant past, and finally falls victim to the lineal time she has resisted all her life.[13] (McMurray 1977: 78-79)

Just as Úrsula eventually succumbs to linear time, so too does her husband, José Arcadio Buendía. Unlike Úrsula's long drawn-out process of waning, however, José Arcadio Buendía's demise is an abrupt leap

into madness. Significantly, his madness is due not to the corrosive
effects of linearity but to the outright recognition of its futility.

> It is time's refusal to move on that drives José Arcadio Buendía to
> madness, as he seeks some evidence that it is linear, as everyone
> believes. His positivistic mind will not allow him to believe
> anything he cannot "prove," and so when he seeks proof that
> Tuesday is different from Monday, and Wednesday from Tuesday,
> he gets stuck... (McNerney: 22)

In the end, "Jose Arcadio's *anguish* before a static universe... where all is
rigidly determined is converted into a *desire* for a return to the origin, to
a communion with himself in the *illud tempus*..." (Merrel: 68), and
hence he departs into madness.

There is an escape, of course, built into the fabric of García
Márquez's novel that does provide some respite from the onslaught of
linear time. It is the room that Melquíades used to inhabit and in which
Aureliano Babilonia finally manages to interpret the parchments left by
the curious gypsy. As the rest of the house falls into disrepair with the
passage of time, Melquíades' room remains strangely untouched. It held
the same clarity and purity for Aureliano Segundo in his maturity as it
had held for him in his childhood (García Márquez 1970: 289). "The
room, needless to say, is [the] timeless space of memory, domain of
history and literature (García Márquez in his writer's solitude)" (Martin:
109). Among the Buendías, only Colonel Aureliano Buendía "fails to
see Melquíades's room as a mythical realm of timelessness, being aware
only of the dust and debris that have accumulated there over the years"
(McMurray 1977: 81). This is no doubt because the Colonel is not a
literary man and cannot appreciate the timeless quality of the written
word.[14]

As Macondo is swallowed up in the hurricane that ends the novel,
Melquíades' room is the last to be destroyed. Inside, Aureliano
Babilonia is translating the last portions of the family history of the
Buendías left by Melquíades.

> In skipping through Melquíades' book, while outside the wind
> erases Macondo forever, Aureliano perhaps discovers what the
> other reader (the reader) has discovered a while back: that he and
> the room in which he reads are immune to the destructions of time
> because they have always lived in another dimension, that of the
> speaking mirror of a book. A mirror which is also a mirage,

composed of solitude and sudden revelation, but above all of the immortality which the word confers. (Rodríguez Monegal: 150)

Here again is the reflection of the timeless, absolute present so important to Octavio Paz and José Ortega y Gasset. The reader experiences the timeless present outside of the novel, but also exists within a linear time of his own. It is a moment of communion that carries an eloquent indictment of linear time and modernity. Time, the message seems to be, is constitutive of reality; time without periodic regeneration and renewal is death.

REALITY

Time and reality are closely related to each other in the thought of Octavio Paz and the novels of Mario Vargas Llosa and Gabriel García Márquez. Just as European philosophical thought about the theory of modernity treats time and reality as fragmented and disjointed, so too are these subjects presented in the literature of Latin America. Octavio Paz sums the situation up in a way that is as reminiscent of Macondo's passage from mythical to linear time as it is of the biblical expulsion from paradise:

> Our situation resembles that of the neurotic, for whom moral principles and abstract ideas have no practical function except as a defense for his privacy—that is, as a complex system he employs to deceive both himself and others regarding the true meaning of his inclinations and the true character of his conflicts. But when these later are clearly and accurately revealed to him, he must then confront them and resolve them for himself. Much the same thing has happened to us. We have suddenly discovered that we are naked and that we are confronted by an equally naked reality. Nothing can justify us now: we alone can answer the questions reality is asking us. (Paz 1985: 168)

The structure of all of the Vargas Llosa and García Márquez novels considered so far accurately reflects the situation Paz describes. Since the onset of modernity and linear time, reality has had to be rethought. It is no longer something given, but rather something the reader must put together (or create, or recreate) himself from the multiple perspectives and multiple dialogues presented in the fictional narrative (and in life). In Vargas Llosa's novels,

> Reality... presents itself to man as something unintelligible, strange, chaotic. A work of fiction attempts to express this particular condition and also—what is important—it attempts to transcend it, to go beyond it. So what at first sight might seem an obsessive preoccupation with form and technique, with devices that sometimes seem contrived and mechanical, must be interpreted, in the last resort, as an attempt to turn language into an adequate tool to confront a particular reality and to recreate it in its innermost and authentic complexity. (Moreno Turner: 28)

Similarly, García Márquez "is equally concerned with denying narrative authority since the natural extension of multiple perception, multiple points of view in these works is the notion that no one truth exists, that all fact is relative" (Christie: 23).

> Our inability to provide a coherent interpretation, a logical meaning, to the events that so disturb the characters concerned stresses the author's fundamental belief in the impenetrable mystery of life and his mockery of the traditional novel so confident in its resolution of all cause and effect relationships. (Foster: 40)

Both Vargas Llosa and García Márquez, along with many writers of the Latin American "boom" generation, have been caught up in an effort to write what they refer to as a "total novel": one that aspires "to compete with reality on an equal basis, confronting it with an image and qualitatively matching it in vitality, vastness and complexity" (Vargas Llosa 1989: 5). A brief investigation of two of the most ambitious attempts to achieve this literary grail, Vargas Llosa's *Conversation in the Cathedral* and García Márquez's *One Hundred Years of Solitude*, will quickly reveal the radically fragmented reality that each author perceives in the modern world.

The premise of Vargas Llosa's *Conversation in the Cathedral* is the chance meeting of two friends and their subsequent conversation of several hours duration in a bar by the name of "*La Catedral.*" All of the action in Vargas Llosa's immense novel takes place within the dialogue of this conversation.[15] Of course, there are many dialogues within dialogues and "past-presents" and other pseudo-present tenses within the "present" of the immediate dialogue, even some that introduce knowledge and/or perspectives that neither of the two speakers in *La Catedral* could possibly have known, but all these are related within the structural brackets of the conversation in *La Catedral*.

Already the dimensions of Vargas Llosa's project and its depiction of reality are becoming clear. By presenting as immediate the thoughts and perceptions of many people in many different times and places in the history of Peru during the Odría regime,[16] a multiplicity of perspectives on reality and fragments of reality are stirred-up in such a way as to make the reader sense his own version of reality (or put it together) from the many bits and pieces floating around in the narrative. "This multiplicity, this simultaneity, this amplitude is the concept of Conversation... The organization of [Vargas Llosa's] novel, far more than the matter it presents, demonstrates the premises of the society he describes..." (Christ: 30):

> What Vargas Llosa is after is reality and what bothers us in reading
> the novel, what seems terribly complex about the style, is just
> what's terribly complex about reality itself... The novel takes up
> these little moments... as they come. That is a political reality.
> (Rabassa: 21)

By the end of the novel, the reader is vividly aware of the kind of modern reality that Vargas Llosa is reflecting:

> For the reader, vagueness and uncertainty are subjective values that
> arise inevitably when a constant disruption of temporal and spatial
> sequences obscures perception of larger formal designs. Yet, on a
> thematic level, this negation of omniscience on the part of the
> author, demonstrating an unwillingness to give a total interpretation
> of a world seen as multiple and diverse, is itself a statement
> underscoring the relative nature of reality. (Moody: 409)

Furthermore, though the reader may hope for some resolution of the story for the main characters in the novel, none is forthcoming. Reality, unlike the novel, is not something that ever resolves itself like a storybook but rather just keeps rumbling on. The close of the novel is somewhat unsatisfying for readers, but true to the Latin American perception of the modernity of underdevelopment:

> You wait for Ambrosio or Zavala to have been saved in a
> Dostoyevsky ending. And they're not! One goes back to his dogs

and the other goes back to his dog. In that sense, it's a good Latin American novel: it doesn't really end.   They go back to their morass. (Rabassa: 19)

Conversation in the Cathedral remains true to its depiction of reality throughout. It is a picture of reality as relative and subjective, and it is typical of the kind of reality in which all of Vargas Llosa's novels are set, including those that do not share the same kind of fragmented literary technique that makes this novel one of Vargas Llosa's most successful attempts to achieve the "total novel."

One Hundred Years of Solitude has also been identified as worthy of being called a "total novel" in the sense that it aspires to compete with reality on an equal basis by presenting a multitude of realities (or perspectives on reality). According to Mario Vargas Llosa,

> The novel does not leave out any of the levels of reality in which the history of Macondo is recorded: it includes the individual and the collective, the legendary and the historical, the daily and the mythical. (Vargas Llosa 1989: 17)

By the author's own admission, "Every single line in *One Hundred Years of Solitude*... has a starting point in reality. I provide a magnifying glass so readers can understand reality better" (Playboy: 74).[17]

The "magnifying glass" of which García Márquez is fond of speaking is best employed in the author's use of the style that critics call "magic realism." This is a style in which normal, everyday events are treated as extraordinary, and fantastic events are related as common occurrences. The famous passages relating to José Arcadío Buendía's discovery of ice (García Márquez 1970: 25-26)[18] and José Arcadio's death (García Márquez 1970: 129-130)[19] are two well-known examples of magic realism.

In the first passage, a perfectly mundane item, ice, is presented against the spectacular backdrop of a troop of gypsies and all the trappings of a pirate's treasure trove. The second passage, by contrast, hides a mysterious death and an extraordinary trail of blood within the banal, matter-of-fact language of the metro page. "The seemingly objective eye which views this reality and the detached, seemingly uninvolved voice which reports it merely add to the breakdown of objective reality, undercutting belief in a continuing, universally accepted physical world" (Levitt: 79). Thus the author's desire to breach the normal boundaries of physical reality in order to present a "total" picture of human reality is accomplished.

> García Márquez's treatment of José Arcadio's death and José Arcadio Buendía's discovery of ice illustrates his method of making the fantastic seem real and the real fantastic, thus eliminating the barrier between objective and imaginary realities and creating a total fictional universe. The role of the practical-minded Úrsula in the [second] episode lends a note of down-to-earth realism to her son's incredible death, just as her flighty husband's role in the [first] episode changes ice into an object of wonder. One can only conclude that reality is relative, elusive, and at times even contradictory, its authenticity depending on the eyes of the viewer or the vantage point from which it is presented. (McMurray 1977: 90)

"Some critics have argued that the Magic Realism of García Márquez is fundamentally different from the narrative art of other writers—a product, this is, not of 'organization,' as in the case of Vargas Llosa, but rather of 'pure invention'" (Levitt: 73). But this argument, whatever its merits in other contexts, misses the point that both narrative techniques are intended to communicate the same fundamental message about modern reality. García Márquez views modern reality in much the same way that Vargas Llosa does: as relative and subjective.

There are other ways in which García Márquez makes clear his understanding of modern reality. One has to do with the banana workers strike related in chapter fifteen. When union leaders come up with a list of demands against the banana company, its owner, Mr. Brown, at first leaves town. A while later Mr. Brown is discovered and forced to sign a copy of the demands. Nevertheless, the next day his lawyers are able to show that the man who signed the demands (and now sat in the courtroom) was not in fact Mr. Jack Brown but actually a lifelong resident of Macondo named Dagoberto Fonseca (García Márquez 1970: 279).[20] Still later...

> In order to foil the strikers and cloud the issue, the company lawyers produce Mr. Brown's death certificate "proving" that he has been run over by a fire engine in Chicago. The workers eventually take their case to a higher court only to be told by the "sleight-of-hand lawyers" that their demands have no validity. It

> seems that the banana company does not have, never has had, and
> never will have any workers in its service because they have all
> been hired on a temporary basis and therefore, by solemn decree of
> the court, "the workers did not exist." (McMurray 1977: 97-98)

Obviously, reality is not something that exists beyond the reach of the
law.

A strike is eventually called by the union leaders, and it culminates
in a massacre of the striking workers. The massacre is witnessed by
José Arcadio Segundo, who himself only narrowly escapes death. He
wakes up in a train car full of corpses (including men, women and
children) and manages to leap from the moving train and make his way
back to Macondo. The train is said to be almost two hundred cars long
and running without lights (García Márquez 1970: 284-285).[21]

A most shocking affront to truth arises from this massacre because,
when José Arcadio Segundo returns to town, he finds that no one
believes his account of what happened. When he confronts other
residents they merely shake their heads and pity him, thinking that he is
mistaking his nightmares for reality (García Márquez 1970: 285, 287).[22]
Under the cover of this blithe and universally believed denial (except for
José Arcadio Segundo), the soldiers are able finally to exterminate the
union leaders one by one.

The malleability of reality in the hands of political power is a
subject that García Márquez returns to again and again. Ironically, he
also sees an example of the same kind of ability to alter reality at work
in his own writing. Speaking of a factual occurrence that helped to
inspire the fictional account of the massacre of the striking workers
recounted above, he says...

> There were not 3000 dead, of course. There were very few
> deaths... Now when they talk about it in the newspapers, even once
> in the congress, they speak about the 3000 who died! And I wonder
> if, with time, it will become true that 3000 were killed. That is why,
> in The Autumn of the Patriarch, there is a moment when the
> Patriarch says, "It doesn't matter if it is not true now; it will be with
> time." (Playboy 1983: 76)

Another, more humorous commentary on modern reality in *One
Hundred Years of Solitude* is provided by and around José Arcadio
Buendía's scientific attempts to learn about reality.

Just as José Arcadío substituted some of the ingredients in the alchemist's laboratory, dooming the process to failure, he uses concrete modern technology to prove abstractions: he refuses to believe in God unless he can capture an image of him with his daguerreotype. The technology of the movies enchants the people from the town until they become aware of its fiction, or rather its lack of literalness. When an actor whose death they lament in one film reappears safe and sound in the next, they destroy the theater. (McNerney: 36)

However García Márquez decides to tell his story, the results are always the same: modern reality is illusive and subjective. José Arcadio is eventually driven mad by the knowledge, but he is also seen to accept and even rise above the chaos:

In death José Arcadio Buendía... transcends the physical and the commonplace through the intensity of his solitary, lifelong struggle to unravel the mysteries of the universe. The significance of his achievements becomes evident through his emergence as a universal archetype, his mythical stature having been assured by his Promethean fate of being tied to the chestnut tree (Prometheus was enchained for defying the laws of the gods), the fantastic rain of flowers proclaiming his death, and the return of his ghost to preserve his descendants' memory of him as the founding patriarch. (McMurray 1977: 83)

LIFE AS THE PRESENT MOMENT

The works of Octavio Paz, Mario Vargas Llosa, and Gabriel García Márquez portray time and reality in much the same way that these concepts are understood within the European theory of modernity. Time is fragmented, reality is subjective, and both are easily manipulated and relative to other concerns.

In Contrast to the European thought surrounding the theory of modernity, however, Octavio Paz has suggested that an escape may be found in the "absolute present" of what he calls "original time." He goes on to explain that this "absolute present" may be humanity's best hope of finding a more healthy reality than the one that we now inhabit. "The search for the present is not the pursuit of an earthly paradise or of a timeless eternity; it is the search for reality" (Paz 1990: 16).

The reality that Paz seeks in the bosom of original time is reminiscent of José Ortega y Gasset's existential philosophy. All of the major ideas that make up Ortega y Gasset's philosophical legacy to Latin America (personal scope, immediacy, continual struggle, and dignity in life) are reflected in Paz's conception of the absolute present. Although original time is characterized by solidarity and community with others, the struggle to achieve this state of mind in the face of modernity—and stay above the waves—is an individual struggle (personal scope). It is also a struggle that must be waged every day without hope for any final victory (continual struggle), though its neglect is sure to bring catastrophe on an individual (immediacy). Finally, human happiness (dignity in life) is the promise held out by Paz's absolute present.[23] Each of these ideas may also be found in the fiction of Mario Vargas Llosa and Gabriel García Márquez, insofar as they also portray versions of original time and the absolute present.

The reality pictured in these works of fiction is not merely a Latin American reality. *One Hundred Years of Solitude* may be "a metaphor for Latin America" as García Márquez says (Playboy: 74), but it is also a metaphor for the reality of modernity itself: "a reality... that lives within us and determines each instant of our countless daily deaths, and that nourishes a source of insatiable creativity, full of sorrow and beauty..." (García Márquez 1988a: 89).

> This is not only an exclusively Latin American reality: it is a spiral of concentric circles, the first of which would be a family with characters more or less extravagant, the second the tiny town of Aracataca with its myths and problems, the third Colombia, the fourth Latin America and the last one, humanity. (Vargas Llosa 1989: 18)

In the literature inspired by this far-flung reality of modernity, "there clearly emerges an indictment of the stifling impulses of the modern age and of the insidious mechanisms by which society creates its victims" (McMurray 1977: 106). There also emerges a general consensus that the key to achieving a better reality in the modern world may be found somewhere within the conception of the absolute present. Of course, a return to the mythical time of a primitive age based on the natural regenerative cycle of seasonal renewal is not possible, at least not beyond the realm of poetry and literature. Still, something may be gleaned from this idea.

The most important difference between the reality of modernity and the reality of Paz's "absolute present" is the way each one is predisposed to create either solitude or solidarity in its proponents. For Paz as well as the other Latin American authors being considered here this opposition deserves greater study for it might be able to open the door to more forward-looking ways of dealing with the problems introduced by modernity.

---

1. For the original Spanish text, see Paz, 1978, page 439.

2. See pages 5-24 for a review of the characteristic transformations of modernity.

3. *Mi tiempo, el tiempo del jardín, la higuera, los juegos con los amigos, el sopor bajo el sol de las tres de la tarde entre las yerbas... —era un tiempo ficticio. A pesar del testimonio de mis sentidos, el timepo de allá, el de los otros, era el verdadero, el tiempo del presente real. Acepté lo inaceptable: fui adulto. Así comenzó mi expulsión del presente.* (Paz 1990: 49)

4. *La fiesta es algo más que una fecha o un aniversario. No celebra, sino reproduce un suceso: abre en dos al tiempo cronométrico para que, por espacio de unas breves horas inconmensurables, el presente eterno se reinstale. La fiesta vuelve creador al tiempo. La repetición se vuelve concepción. El timepo engendra. La Edad de Oro regresa.* (Paz 1959: 189)

5. "The sterility of the bourgeois world will end in suicide or a new form of creative participation. This is the 'theme of our times,' in Ortega y Gasset's phrase" (Paz 1985: 212).

6. *La ciudad y los perros* (1963), *La casa verde* (1966), and *Conversación en La Catedral* (1969).

7. Dick Gerdes names it "the technique of interpolating dialogues" (Gerdes: 69) and Sara Castro-Klarén refers to it as "the technique called assimilated dialogue" (Castro-Klarén: 65). Their meanings are the same as Williams', but most critics have found the "telescope" image more attractive.

8. The comments of Gregory Rabassa, translator of *The Green House* and *Conversation in the Cathedral*, are instructive: "Vargas Llosa doesn't really change tenses; he changes times. It's the old problem of the aspects of the verb. I am not thinking so much of grammar, then, as of the temporal point of view" (Rabassa: 17).

9. It is interesting to note that *The Green House* actually began as two separate novels. Vargas Llosa, complaining that he could not keep the characters from travelling between the stories, eventually combined them into one (Diez: 1978).

10. Consider Mary Davis' statement, which highlights the difficulties critics

have had in trying to reconcile this highly abstract quality of Vargas Llosa's novels with his otherwise very realistic style: "Critics have always sensed that aspects of the ambiguity of the Peruvian's texts arise from the combination of realistic elements of style with something else. Finding a term adequate to designate the other aspect has led to a minor polemic over whether or not the term "mythic" should be employed with Vargas Llosa's peculiar verbal world" (Davis, M.: 136).

11. *Cien Años de Soledad* (1967), *El Otono del Patriarca* (1975), and *Crónica de una muerte anunciada* (1981).

12. Paz suggests that the myth of the golden age "is neither in nature nor in history but between them: [it is] at that moment when men establish their grouping with an agreement which, at the same time, unites them with each other and ties the group with the natural world"(Paz, quoted in Sims: 142).

13. Úrsula's destruction is a consequence of the demise of cyclical time in Macondo. An interesting symbol of this relationship is provided in the passage quoted here. Aureliano Babilonia, the mischievous great-great-great-great-grandson who treats Úrsula as a plaything in her old age, will one day become the translator of Melquíades' parchments, representing the final triumph of reason over myth and tradition.

14. Note that the soldiers who come to arrest Arcadio Segundo were also unable to perceive the timeless qualities of Melquíades' room (García Márquez 1970: 288-289).

15. The original Spanish version of the novel was published in two volumes. The English translation is in one large volume of over six hundred pages.

16. The Odría dictatorship lasted from 1948 to 1956 and corresponds to the time period covered in *Conversation in the Cathedral*.

17. Often García Márquez's "starting point in reality" can be rather bizarre. The reality behind the ghost of Prudencio Aguilar in *One Hundred Years of Solitude*, for example, may go back to García Márquez's childhood memories of his grandfather: "The grandfather had a devil who haunted him: he had once killed a man. He would take his grandson to the circus and, quite suddenly, he would stop in the street and exclaim: 'Oh! You don't know how much a dead body weighs'" (Vargas Llosa 1988: 7). García Márquez's own reputation for premonitions, his fear of "pava" (a kind of jinx that attaches to certain things), and his belief in the magical qualities of yellow flowers may also be revealing in this respect (see Mendoza and García Márquez: 111-117).

18. For the original spanish text, see García Márquez 1967, pages 21-22.

19. For the original Spanish text see García Márquez 1967: page 110.

20. For the original Spanish text see García Márquez 1967: page 237.

21. For the original Spanish text see García Márquez 1967: pages 241-242.

22. For the original Spanish text, see García Márquez 1967: pages 242 & 244.

23. See chapter 3 for a more extensive discussion of these elements of Ortega y Gasset's philosophical legacy for Latin America.

CHAPTER 6

Solitude and Love

> *Solitude is the profoundest fact of the human
> condition. Man is the only being who knows he
> is alone, and the only one who seeks out
> another.*[1]
>
> Octavio Paz (1985: 195)
> *The Labyrinth of Solitude*

In Latin America, as elsewhere, the critique of culture in modernity focuses on the modern way of life. The "self" is at the center of this controversy, for the weakening of the self is the most important consequence of the cultural problem of modernity. The iron cage of modern economics, the separation of the value spheres, and the awesome power of rational 'systems' in modernity are all cultural forces that tend to separate and isolate individual selves from each other and prevent growth (see chapter 2, pp. 32-36). Without any positive dynamic toward the deepening and broadening of the internal scope of the self in modernity, individual selves become detached from the life of the community and turn inward on themselves. The result is a profound and widespread sense of isolation and the feeling of quiet desperation so characteristic of modern individuals: the "dead stare" characteristic of "normal" adulthood in modernity.[2]

In Latin America, the crisis of the self in modernity is reflected in the concept of "solitude." Many authors use this theme to characterize the modernity of Latin America. Although Europeans and North

Americans also use the concept of solitude to explore the culture of modernity, it is a term that is particularly well suited to Latin America.

The real contribution of Latin American writers to the philosophical discourse of modernity may not be their uniquely intense comprehension of solitude, however, so much as their understanding of the importance of love. As a radical negation of solitude, love carries the promise of renewal and communion. Though passionate love may not ignite more than a momentary burst of the wonder of Paz's absolute present, it could suggest more enduring ways of dealing with the cultural problem of modernity. The second half of this chapter explores love and its possibilities for contributing to a renewed sense of self in modernity.

The cultural problem of modernity will almost certainly not be overcome simply through a renewed appreciation for love in society. Nevertheless, if the isolation of the self in modernity can be mitigated through an infusion of love, then that is all that can be hoped in any event. José Ortega y Gasset's vision of the shipwrecked sailor is built on nothing more promising than the effort to continue to tread water for a little while longer. The Latin American return to love is no more than this; it is the "swimming stroke" of a struggling culture not ready to let itself drown.

SOLITUDE

The theme of solitude is not new to Latin American literature. As early as Domingo Faustino Sarmiento's *Facundo* it had already appeared as a major part of the self-understanding of Latin Americans. Since then, the concept has grown with the region:

> Solitude in Sarmiento's *Facundo* is geographic isolation... As the Latin American novel gradually turned away from its preoccupation with the land and the rural setting and more toward man himself in the twentieth-century urban setting, the theme of solitude ceased to be a simple problem of rivers, mountains, and plains and, by the 1950s, had become a chronic sociological and psychological problem seen as having its roots in the period of Conquest and as still exerting its influence today. (Feustle: 522)

For Octavio Paz, the fundamental cause of solitude is division of one from another: "Every separation causes a wound... Any break (with ourselves or those around us, with the past or the present) creates a feeling of solitude" (Paz 1985: 64). But Latin American solitude, the solitude of modernity, is far deeper than simple separation. In Paz's thought, it is presented as a mythical separation from original wholeness, or from original time, as discussed in the previous chapter. Paz clearly believes that modern life is a search for the secret ways that might lead back to this original lost wholeness:

> It is true that the feeling of separation is universal and not peculiar to Spanish Americans. It is born at the very moment of our births: as we are wrenched from the Whole, we fall into a foreign land. This never-healing wound is the unfathomable depth of every man. All our ventures and exploits, all our acts and dreams, are bridges designed to overcome the separation and reunite us with the world and our fellow beings. Each man's life and the collective history of humanity can thus be seen as an attempt to reconstruct the original situation. An unfinished and endless cure for our divided condition. (Paz 1990: 10-11)[3]

Though Paz's poetic description of humanity's mythical separation from original wholeness may seem detached from the reality of everyday modern solitude, he provides another, less lofty, approach to his thesis. Speaking of solitude as a condition characteristic of certain periods of people's lives, he paints a picture of modern solitude that many would recognize as a reflection of their own lives:

> Solitude is not characteristic of maturity. When a man struggles with other men or with things, he forgets himself in his work, in creation or in the construction of objects, ideas and institutions. His personal consciousness unites with that of others: time takes on meaning and purpose and thus becomes history, a vivid, significant account with both a past and a future. Our singularity—deriving from the fact that we are situated in time, in a particular time which is made up of our own selves and which devours us while it feeds us—is not actually abolished, but it is attenuated and, in a certain sense, "redeemed." Our personal existence takes part in history, which becomes, in Eliot's phrase, "a pattern of timeless moments." During vital and productive epochs, therefore, a mature man suffering from the illness of solitude is always an anomaly. This type of solitary figure is very frequent today, and indicates the gravity of our ills. In an epoch of group work, group songs, group pleasures, man is more alone than ever. Modern man never surrenders himself to what he is doing. A part of him—the

profoundest part—always remains detached and alert. Man spies on himself. Work, the only modern god, is no longer creative. It is endless, infinite work, corresponding to the inconclusive life of modern society. And the solitude it engenders—the random solitude of hotels, offices, shops and movie theaters—is not a test that strengthens the soul, a necessary purgatory. It is utter damnation, mirroring a world without exit. (Paz 1985: 204)[4]

Thus the modern person is not just alone—separated from other people—but solitary in a generic sense: undifferentiated, leveled (in Simmel's [1978] sense), an abstraction without singularity. The modern worker, undifferentiated in both his social class and his economic activity, is Paz's best example of this unwholesome solitude:

The modern worker lacks individuality. The class is stronger than the individual and his personality dissolves in the generic. That is the first and gravest mutilation a man suffers when he transforms himself into an industrial wage earner... His efforts, unlike those of a doctor, an engineer or a carpenter, cannot be distinguished from those of other men. The abstraction that characterizes him—work measured by time—does not separate him from other abstractions. On the contrary, it binds him to them. (Paz 1985: 67)[5]

But if modern people would recognize this image as one of unwholesome solitude, they might be less familiar with the kind of solitude that Paz would characterize as a healthy part of human existence. This healthy form of solitude is the kind that "invites introspection" or "appears as a challenge": a "spur to action, to go forth into the outside world and encounter others" (Paz 1990: 10). It is the solitude that is the necessary other half of communion (the unity or "wholeness" of which Paz speaks so lovingly). "History" in Paz's thought is "a dialectic (or rhythm) of solitude and communion, the ebb and flow of liberation/imprisonment, the *instante* and empty sequential time" (Wilson: 54).

The "dialectic of solitude," as Paz (1959) calls it, is the play between (healthy) solitude and communion with others that Paz sees as a necessary pattern of human life. When this dialectic is broken, as in modernity, the result is a kind of unredeemable solitude with symptoms that resemble those that Durkheim feared might result from an elimination of "the sacred" in modern society. Here "solitude" can be seen as an important part of the Latin American experience of the cultural problem of modernity. García Márquez interprets solitude in much the same way as Paz, while Vargas Llosa seems to focus on a more distinctly Latin American aspect of modern solitude.

Solitude is an important theme in many of García Márquez's novels, though it appears most strongly in *One Hundred Years of Solitude* and *The Autumn of the Patriarch*. Nevertheless, García Márquez is not always clear about what he means when invoking this illusive concept. Sometimes he suggests that it means a kind of anti-solidarity:

> Solitude, I believe, is the opposite of solidarity. (Mendoza and García Márquez: 75)

But at other times he has used it to mean differentness or strangeness:

> When García Márquez, receiving the Nobel Prize, spoke of the solitude of Latin America... he meant its difference, its strangeness to others, and the failure of supposedly friendly countries to offer concrete support to its aspirations. It is true that he also took pride in what he saw as the source of this difference, the extravagant unlikeliness of much of life in Latin America, but this is precisely the reverse side of the same coin. Solitude is like progress: one always has too much or too little. (Wood: 34)

Clearly, "solitude" (or *soledad*) is a word that deserves close attention. On the one hand, it is true that García Márquez must find the attraction of solitude (or quietism) a dangerous temptation for politically disaffected or despairing intellectuals in Latin America (Wood: 36). But on the other hand,

> Solitude seems not an entirely bad thing for Márquez... Melquíades' chronicling of the story, and the subsequent deciphering of it, both depend on a willed seclusion. Writing is a homeopathic form of solitude which serves an ultimate purpose of solidarity. (M. Bell: 68)

García Márquez's own profession is thus at least partially distinguished by solitude according to his own confession. "There is no more solitary profession than writing, in the sense that when you're writing no one can help you, nor can anybody really know what it is you're trying to do. You're absolutely alone, totally isolated, with a blank page in front of you" (Mendoza and García Márquez: 89).

Through comments like these, it becomes clear that solitude has both positive and negative forms (or manifestations) for García Márquez in much the same sense that it did for Octavio Paz. Michael Wood's comments are enlightening:

> It is worth pausing over the word. *Soledad* is an alluring, mournful, much-used Spanish noun, suggesting both a doom and a solace, a flight from love but also from lies, a claim to dignity which is also a submission to neglect. *Loneliness* has some of this flavor, but only some. *Soledad* is part of a culture which calls its streets paradise or bitterness or disenchantment; and gives girls names like Virtues, Sorrows and Mercies. Soledad is itself a girl's name... (Wood: 34)

The "double edge" of solitude, its healthy and unhealthy forms, is not nearly as clear in García Márquez as it is in Paz. This may have been the author's intention, though a more likely explanation is that the other side of solitude, its healthy manifestation, simply crept into the story and characters through the poetic imagination. In either case, two of García Márquez's most solitary characters, the Patriarch and Colonel Aureliano Buendía, illuminate the presence of both of these manifestations of solitude in his work.

When asked how he would define *The Autumn of the Patriarch*, García Márquez said "as a poem on the solitude of power" (Mendoza and García Márquez: 86). It is an apt description, for the patriarch is an archetypal depiction of the victim of the peculiar kind of solitude that comes with power.

The solitude of power is a completely unhealthy form of solitude, in Paz's sense, because it is based not just on separation from others but the complete immersion of the self in itself. The entire external environment, including other people and basic physical realities, is manipulated to conform with the patriarch's personal wishes and desires. His power was so great that time itself would be set according to his command (García Márquez 1976: 86-87). The patriarch's power reaches god-like proportions. He is said to create history according to the designs of his own will and make it legitimate in the eyes of the nation, no matter how outlandish a lie it was when it began (García Márquez 1976: 159).[6]

The extent of the patriarch's ingrown self and narcissism is represented in the person of Patricio Aragonés, his perfect double. Aragonés' body is altered to perfectly match the patriarch's in every respect, even to the point of flattening his feet, rupturing a testicle, and forcing him to forget how to read and write (García Márquez 1976: 28).

> He not only serves a decoy against all possible assassination attempts, but also is joined symbiotically with the patriarch, helping the latter to withstand the imagined threats to, and cast off the burden of, his fragmented self ("...he had clung to Patricio Aragonés as if he were himself... they spent entire afternoons... counting swallows like two decrepit lovers... so apart from the world that he himself [the patriarch] failed to realize that his fierce struggle to exist twice [i. e. his struggle to overcome his fear of self-annihilation through self-duplication and the projection of his fragmented self onto another] only nursed the contrary suspicion that he was existing less and less..." [i. e., he was experiencing the terrifying loss of self]). (McMurray 1977: 130-131)

It is this feeling of "existing less and less" and the accompanying loss of self that is the outcome of the solitude of power, for what the patriarch's overwhelming power does is obliterate his sense of self. To become like God is to have no equal—no other. But without any "other" to give it meaning, there can be no self. Thus, by the end of his life, the patriarch does not remember who he is when death appears and calls him by his given name. "He has too tinkered with facts and perceptions, at the same time playing such contradictory roles over the years—patriarch to the people and devoted son to his mother, commander of everything within the country and puppet to foreign forces—that... he has lost track of his own reality" (McNerney: 57).

The results of the solitude exhibited here, the political solitude of the patriarch, are characteristic of all forms of what Paz would call unhealthy solitude. Though in the case of the patriarch solitude arises from the experience of too much power, there is in fact a deeper cause that lies behind all forms of unhealthy solitude. It is the failure to achieve meaningful communication with other people, the failure to (as Paz would have it) return to the experience of oneness with others. As happens with other forms of solitude that do not act as a "spur to action, to go forth into the outside world and encounter others" (Paz 1990: 10), the solitude of power in the end leads only to "a great masturbation" (McNerney: 56) and the patriarch eventually ends his life as a "solitary drowned man" (an image that invokes Ortega y Gasset).

Colonel Aureliano Buendía is another famous solitary figure from García Márquez's fiction. He is perhaps the most memorable character in *One Hundred Years of Solitude,* and he also appears or exists in the background of a number of García Márquez's other works.[7]   The Colonel's solitude is perhaps the most acute of any of the Buendías, but, unlike the patriarch whose solitude is absolute, Colonel Aureliano Buendía's solitude exists on a more human scale. He exhibits both healthy and unhealthy forms of solitude (in Paz's sense), though he is eventually overcome by the latter. For this reason the Colonel can be seen as a kind of tragic figure, both more believable to readers than the patriarch and more telling as a critique of the solitude of modernity.

Even before his birth, readers of *One Hundred Years of Solitude* begin to learn about the character of Colonel Aureliano Buendía. Úrsula wakes one night late in her pregnancy to the sound of the baby weeping inside her womb. She takes it as an unmistakable sign that the child will suffer from an inability to experience love (García Márquez 1970: 233). Everyone is amazed when the Colonel is born with his eyes open (García Márquez 1970: 168), and many special powers or oddities are attributed to him throughout his life:

> He can see the present and the immediate future, he reads minds,
> sees through his own and other people's illusions. He can picture,
> we are told, both sides of his thought [133]. He can't see the
> splintered, retarded time in Melquíades' room, the magical release
> from dust and decay, but when Melquíades finally vanishes and the
> room succumbs to change, it is eerily said to be the room Aureliano
> had foreseen [331]. Even his blindness is a form of sight: the
> problem is the misery of what he perceives, the wintry triumph of
> his lucidity. (Wood: 101)

Úrsula's judgment about Aureliano's incapacity to love may not have been wholly correct, at least not in his younger days. He writes poetry as an adolescent, falls in love with Remedios Moscote, and even when he decides to go to war against the conservatives his reasons are impeccably moral:

> Aureliano doesn't understand "how people arrived at the extreme of
> waging war over things that could not be touched with the hand"
> [97]. He is... unmoved by abstractions but provoked by cruelty, by
> the sight of victimization... In fact Aureliano's position is not a
> political one at all, but a moral response to a political world, and
> many ambiguities in the novel revolve around our feelings about this
> response. (Wood: 94)

In a turning point of his life, Colonel Aureliano Buendía returns to his poetry and begins to understand himself. While recovering from a near-fatal dose of poisoned coffee, he wakes in the bedroom of his dead wife (who, in happier times, used to bring coffee to him out in the workshop) and decides to take up writing again. In his verses he is able to see that his revolutionary fighting is futile. He decides that his own Liberal party can have no real meaning for anyone (presumably because it cannot change the sad and immoral nature of modern reality) and tells his friend he realizes that he is only fighting because of pride (García Márquez 1970: 133).[8] Clearly, this is the admission of someone who has seen into the abyss of modernity. The Colonel, with his wide-open eyes, sees reality as the twenty-first century sees reality; values are relative, truth is subjective, meaning is equivocal, and nihilism everywhere. What reason for action is left besides self-centered pride?

Michael Wood has presented a masterful reading of Colonel Aureliano Buendía's character based on these insights (Wood 1990). His work is worthy of a rather long excerpt. Speaking of his military opponent, José Raquel Moncada, a man whose government Úrsula judges to have been the best Macondo ever had (García Márquez 1970: 153), Wood comments that Aureliano...

> is unbendingly honest and principled, willing to have this same opponent [Moncada] executed, although he likes and admires him, because "it's the Revolution" that is doing the shooting, and the other man would have done the same in his place [153]. But there is certainly a stoppage of feelings in Aureliano, and some self-deception: *we are reading a fable about the corruption of incorruption* [my emphasis]. When Aureliano looks at José Raquel, the man he is about to have killed, he sees him "with his heart": "he was startled to see how much he had aged, how his hands shook, and the rather routine air of acceptance ["*la conformidad un poco rutinaria*"] with which he awaited death, and then he felt a profound contempt for himself which he took for the beginnings of pity." This is an extraordinary insight, but kept just beyond the reach of the character. Aureliano despises the depth of his own mistake. A man who didn't recognize abstractions is about to have an abstraction kill a man he would rather keep alive. But even now Aureliano himself doesn't understand his own response. he feels the self-contempt but thinks it is pity. His heart is in worse shape than he thinks. (Wood: 96)

Wood calls Colonel Aureliano Buendía's story a "fable about the corruption of incorruption." It is also a fable about not so much an inability to experience love (as Úrsula would have it) but a fear of loving too much within an all too precarious and relentless reality.[9] Every time the Colonel suffers a significant personal loss in the novel his reaction is not sorrow, but rage combined with an exasperating recognition of his own impotence (García Márquez 1970: 226)[10]

> Surely we see a man who is chronically afraid of feeling, romantically risks it, and retreats into cold fury when calamity occurs. Aureliano's response is the same when sixteen of his sons are massacred, a "dull anger", "*una cólera sorda*", which puts a frightening glint back into his eyes—of the kind that at other times made chairs move just because he looked at them [212: 226-227].
> (Wood: 97)

The solitude of Colonel Aureliano Buendía begins as the kind of healthy solitude that Paz says is necessary in order to experience its opposite, the communion and redemption of love. The Colonel does, after all, "risk" love. His fault—his tragedy—is that he cannot recover from the unjust losses inflicted on him by reality; the continuing losses that his clear sight of future reality tells him are sure to come. Why care at all then?

Colonel Aureliano Buendía's thirty-two armed uprisings began with his anger against injustice, but after the sound and fury of that is past he admits that all he is fighting for is his own pride. He knows now that he cannot change the nature of the world (the nature of reality) by force of arms. There is a metaphor of the Enlightenment here. Enlightened reason and science alone will never eliminate the capricious injustices of the world. The twenty-first century is ready to face this fact, much as the Colonel faces it in his old age. Seen in this light, his thirty-two armed uprisings were unwinnable from the start.

The story of the twenty-first century is yet to be played out, but the Colonel's fable ends a dismal tragedy. In many ways the strongest and most farseeing character in the novel, arguably the most fully modern, Colonel Aureliano Buendía is conquered by his own knowledge. The mask he put on to protect his "self" from the pain of the world has become his prison.

> The dryness of Aureliano's heart, the coldness of his entrails which is said to be a source of vitality [151], are both a mask and a desolate achievement—since the mask can no longer be lifted or distinguished from the face. (Wood: 97)

Like Macbeth, by the end of his years the Colonel sees life as "a tale told by an idiot, full of sound and fury, signifying nothing" (Shakespeare 1956: 105). The Colonel's equivalent to Macbeth's "poor player" is his vision of a passing circus parade on the last day of his life. He stands in front of his house and watches elephants, clowns, dancing bears and other entertainers pass by, and then is confronted by the silence and solitude after the parade. He tries to remember the sound and fury of the event as he leans his head on the chestnut tree and relieves himself, but quickly loses the memory. In death, his head is pulled in between his shoulders and the family doesn't even notice he is gone until the next morning when the vultures attract their attention (García Márquez 1970: 250).[11]

Colonel Aureliano Buendía has pulled his head in between his shoulders ever since he realized that his armed uprisings were futile. He is defeated by the impotence of his solitude just as the incorruptible champions of modern rationalism will be defeated by their solitude unless a new, more confidently spirited way of living can be found. At the end of his life he cannot remember his life. At the end of the book, the only evidence of his passing is a street sign.

> He can't remember, isn't remembered. He is not the most necessary character in the book, but he is the most missed, the one we most need to understand. He is the first human being to be born in Macondo, and his humanity, however tenuous and chilled, is important. He is the novel's dark conscience. No wonder García Márquez was reluctant to have him die, and went upstairs trembling, he says, when he had written the words [quoted above]. His wife Mercedes knew at once what had happened. "The colonel's dead," she said, and García Márquez himself lay on his bed and cried for two hours. (Wood: 102)

It may seem odd to mourn so heartily the passing of such a distant and unfeeling character as Colonel Aureliano Buendía, but in the end his solitude may be our own.

Solitude does not have the same thunderous presence in Mario Vargas Llosa's works that it has in those of García Márquez, but Vargas

Llosa's appreciation of the theme is no less important. Three of Vargas Llosa's cultural themes in particular are aimed directly at the cultural problem of modernity and may be interpreted as examples of the theme of solitude in Latin American literature: his critique of bureaucracy in *Captain Pantoja and the Special Service* (1978); the analysis of race and class in Peru presented in many of his works, including *The Storyteller* (1989a); and the critique of the code of *hombría* present in all his works, but most notably in *The Time of the Hero* (1966).[12]

Vargas Llosa's most amusing critique of modern culture is presented in *Captain Pantoja and the Special Service*. The story is about a young military man, Captain Pantaleón Pantoja, who has a particular genius for organization.[13] His abilities are noticed by his superiors and he is assigned the task of solving one of the Peruvian military's most embarrassing problems. Citizens living in communities near remote military posts have been complaining about soldiers coming to their towns on leave and raping local women. The solution, as the army sees it, is to establish a "special service" to satisfy the sexual needs of its enlisted personnel. Thus Captain Pantoja, a self-disciplined, third-generation military man of exemplary character, becomes the Peruvian army's pimp-technocrat par excellence.

Beyond the humor of the situation is the author's trenchant critique of bureaucracy and organization in modern life. Vargas Llosa has referred to *Captain Pantoja and the Special Service* as his "parable of an intermediate man" (Christ 1978: 33). Pantaleón Pantoja is the ideal type of the modern technocrat, a model of efficiency and champion of bureaucratic procedure. He sets up the Special Service on the basis of rational procedures and observations of the relevant variables, even to the point of using a stopwatch to time his own sexual relations with his wife for use in his calculations (as related in this letter from his wife to her sister):

> Do you remember how he's always been so formal ever since we got married so you always joked a lot and told me I'm sure with Panta you must be doing without, Pocha? Well, you can't laugh at your brother-in-law anymore in that respect, you bad-mouth, because since he stepped foot in Iquitos he's become a savage... I've told you, I only got him to tend to his business once every ten or fifteen days (how embarrassing to talk to you about this, Chichi) and now the little bandit's excited every two, three days and I have to put the brakes on his passion, because it isn't right, no, really, with this heat and sticky humidity... I have to tell you it makes me

laugh to see your little brother-in-law so horny. Sometimes he's itching to do a little business during the daytime, right after lunch, with the siesta as an excuse, but of course I don't let him, and sometimes he wakes me at dawn with that craziness. Picture this, the other night I caught him with a stopwatch timing how long our business took us. I asked him about it and he got very confused. Later he confessed to me he had to know how long a little business like that took for a normal couple. Do you think he's turning into a pervert? (Vargas Llosa 1978: 50) [14]

As the supreme bureaucrat, Pantoja breaks down all the duties of the Special Service, including the sex act, into their component parts, calculates the time and expenses involved in each part, and generally "deals with the situation as a classic case of scarcity, in which the demand for a commodity (women) and an activity (sexual intercourse) far exceeds the supply" (Kovács: 44). An illuminating discussion of this situation is presented by Katherine S. Kovács (1984). She interprets Pantoja's behavior in terms of György Lukács' concepts of alienation and reification:

> In Peru as elsewhere throughout the world, work activities are organized according to "rational" principles. Managers in factories and in offices conduct time and motion studies bringing in mathematical calculations and even psychological manipulation to facilitate the efficient functioning of their organizations. Both in the factory and in the office, the manager views the worker as an element in the system of mechanized operations. As György Lukács suggested in his *History and Class Consciousness*, the worker's isolation and specialization lead him to see himself in similar terms. Thus the relations between people tend to take on the character of the relation between things. Lukács called this creation of pseudo-things "reification," and saw it as a type of alienation which is accepted and internalized as something natural and normal... It is this structure of unitary consciousness that Vargas Llosa examines in *Pantaleón y las visitadoras*. Pantaleón is the ultimate manager-middleman whose extreme efficiency reflects his total submission to the bureaucratic order. (Kovács: 42)

Insofar as he is the perfect bureaucrat, the "genius clerk," Pantaleón Pantoja represents the incursion of rational organization into all aspects of modern life (a process that was referred to earlier as the trend of "rationalization"). Recall that this trend is not just the movement toward mechanistic procedures and working conditions, but also a way of approaching life...

> which becomes more and more formally rational, of an even more monstrous intensification of unilateral specialization violating the human essence of man... a total submission of the individual bureaucrat to a system of relations between things, [an] idea that his 'honor' and 'sense of responsibility' demand such a submission, all that shows that the division of work has penetrated into ethics. (Lukács, quoted in Kovács: 43)

In this sense then, "Pantaleón... is Marcuse's *One-Dimensional Man*, (Marcuse 1964) molded by his work activities as well as by the superstructural and ideological elements generated by those activities to perform obediently and without question" (Kovács: 47).

The fact that Pantoja's bureaucratization concerns one of the most intimate aspects of human life, sex, is of supreme importance. It is not only the source of humor in *Captain Pantoja and the Special Service*, but also the cutting edge of his critique of the modern lifestyle. In modernity, even sex is subject to rationalization. Now, "one must speak (of sex) as a thing that must not be simply condemned or tolerated, but managed, inserted in systems of utility, regulated... Sex is not only judged, it is administered. It calls for procedures of management and must be taken in hand through analytical discourses" (Foucault: 51). As Kovács concludes, "human beings are assessed as factors in the production and distribution process, and the relations between men and women, even ones of such an intimate nature, are converted into the relation between things—the basis for the process of reification" (Kovács: 44).

One may also see Vargas Llosa as attacking the whole idea of state intervention in the more intimate areas of life activity. Pantoja's activity is, after all, a government effort to control people's behavior through the granting or withholding of sex. (Soldiers are disciplined by having their sexual privileges rescinded.) In this respect the Special Service may be criticized on the basis of Marcuse's idea of 'repressive desublimation'. "The Special Service fosters the control of the state not through prohibition or repression but through intervention in and manipulation of the instinctual side of human life" (Kovács: 45).

Vargas Llosa brings home his critique of this process by telling the story of Pantoja's downfall. The perfect bureaucrat is eventually tempted to violate his own rules by the presence of "The Brazilian," a dark-haired beauty who is depicted as a kind of 'super-whore' by Vargas Llosa. When she is killed by an unlucky bullet in an ambush laid by young toughs from a local village (who are anxious to receive the same services they know the soldiers enjoy), Pantoja is overcome with grief and buries her publicly with full military honors. Of course, once the official nature of the Special Service becomes public knowledge, the military leadership shuts it down and transfers Pantoja to a remote Andean outpost (Peru's equivalent to Siberia).

Captain Pantoja's symbolic role changes during this chain of events. In succumbing to the charms of "The Brazilian," Pantoja is initiated into the values of non-bureaucratic, emotional discourse. He ceases to be the "one-dimensional man" and becomes a composite of two world-views. When he speaks at the Brazilian's funeral in full dress uniform, he is attempting to reconcile these two ethical orders into one system, but the attempt is futile. People simply will not accept the bureaucratization of sex, and, as a now-tainted champion of bureaucracy, Pantoja is exiled by the Army to a remote outpost to "rehabilitate" himself. For Vargas Llosa, rationalization simply cannot be extended to intimate areas of human life without causing an unacceptable loss of humanity:

> Stripped of mystery and of centuries-old religious and moral taboos, as well as of the elaborate rituals that surrounded the practice of it, physical love has come to be the most natural thing in the world for the younger generations, a gymnastic exercise, a temporary diversion, something very different from that central mystery of life, of the approach by way of it to the gates of heaven and hell that it still was for my generation... Perhaps it is a good thing that sex has come to seem something natural to most mortals. To me it never was, nor is it now. Seeing a naked woman in a bed has always been the most disquieting and most disturbing of experiences, something that never would have had for me that transcendental nature, deserving of so much tremulous respect and so much joyous expectation, if sex had not been, in my childhood and adolescence, surrounded by taboos, prohibitions, and prejudices, if in order to make love to a woman there had not been so many obstacles to overcome in those days. (Vargas Llosa 1994: 188-189)[15]

Race and Class divisions are another aspect of Vargas Llosa's critique of modern culture. Here solitude is measured not in terms of bureaucratization and alienation, but in the stratification and isolation of groups.   Vargas Llosa refers to it as "the national disease" [*la enfermedad nacional*]:

> In particolored Peruvian society, and perhaps in all societies which have many races and extreme inequalities, *blanco* and *cholo* are terms that refer to other things besides race or ethnic group: they situate a person socially and economically... One is always *blanco* or *cholo* in relation to someone else, because one is always better or worse situated than others, or one is more or less poor or important, or possessed of more or less Occidental or mestizo or Indian or African or Asiatic features than others, and all this crude nomenclature that decides a good part of any one person's fate is maintained by virtue of an effervescent structure of prejudices and sentiments—disdain,   scorn,   envy,   bitterness,   admiration, emulation—which, many times, beneath ideologies, values, and contempt for values, is the deep-seated explanation for the conflicts and frustrations of Peruvian life. (Vargas Llosa 1994: 5-6)[16]

Many of Vargas Llosa's novels display this racism as it operates in Peruvian society.   Its presence is obvious in *The Time of the Hero*, where it creates status divisions between students at the Leoncio Prado military academy.   Jum's downfall in *The Green House* is another example.   Its effects are everywhere in *Conversation in the Cathedral*, in which all interpersonal relations are conditioned by one's social status. Even *Captain Pantoja and the Special Service* does not escape, as "Pantaleón is, above all, a *cholito*":

> If Pantaleón had been more of a criollo, if he had come from a slightly higher social class to begin with, he would have contrived not to accept his assignment.   He would have suspected that the whole idea of providing safe and adequate sexual satisfaction for the army troops based in the Amazon jungle was by definition an impossible task. (Castro-Klarén: 137, 138)

In *Aunt Julia and the Scriptwriter*,[17] the divisions caused by race are interrelated with those set up by cultural taboos against incest. As in *One Hundred Years of Solitude*, incest is a symbol of solitude because it represents an unwillingness to break out of the family circle.   In *Aunt Julia*, the barrier of the family circle seems almost insurmountable:

> All twenty episodes tell family stories triangulated on the basis of transgressions of the kinship code, that in turn harbor the

transgression of the identity code predicated by kinship. Marito, the adolescent son, grandson, and nephew in the Llosa family, becomes Varguitas, the independent husband and brother-in-law by virtue of his marriage to his aunt Julia. Upon his return from Paris, and by virtue of his marriage to cousin Patricia and his success as a novelist, Varguitas becomes Mario Vargas Llosa, grandson of the same grandfather, son and nephew-in-law of his Uncle Lucho and his Aunt Olga, and former husband of his aunt Julia Urquidi. (Castro-Klarén: 156-157)

The triangular incestuous relations that make up the soap-opera world of Pedro Camacho are even more confused: eventually even the identities of characters become mixed up with each other and the impossibly disoriented scriptwriter collapses into madness.

A related but different exploration of the divisions between people created by culture is presented in Vargas Llosa's *The Storyteller*. This absorbing novel presents autobiographical sketches of the narrator/author's friendship with Saúl Zuratas, an anthropologist and fellow student doing field research on the Machiguenga tribe in the Amazon Basin of Peru, together with alternating chapters in which an *hablador*, a Machiguenga "speaker" or cultural "storyteller," tells of the beliefs and customs of the Machiguenga tribe. The narrator of the autobiographical sketches informs us that he doesn't feel he can "write about the hablador because to do so he would have to be a Machiguenga... He does not write because, according to his ideal of realism, he can only write by getting rid of his Western mentality and becoming an hablador" (Acosta Cruz: 135). The authorship of the alternating *hablador* chapters is thus put in doubt, and this creates the tension essential to the novel's cultural theme.

The reader is never informed unequivocally of the identity of the *hablador* speaking in the alternate chapters, but by the end of the novel it is clear that the storyteller is Saúl Zuratas, who has abandoned Peruvian society to become a Machiguenga himself.

> The paradox of the novel is that even though Vargas Llosa doubts the wisdom and truthfulness of Zuratas' position, the novel itself builds a test case in which the culture of the Machiguengas referred to as primitive by Vargas Llosa himself emerges as a self-sufficient, highly civilized, and enduring human construct...
>
> By proposing the story of Zuratas' transformation into the *hablador*, Vargas Llosa vitiates the entire argument on behalf of the

cultural self-sufficiency of the Machiguengas. Since the *hablador* is in fictional fact Zuratas, and Zuratas is a modern, trained anthropologist, it would follow that no authentic *hablador* could have rendered the Machiguenga memory and discourse in as orderly or fascinating a narrative as Zuratas/the *hablador* does in the pages of *El hablador*. (Castro-Klarén: 219-220)

But there is a deeper paradox in this story, one that strikes more near the mark of solitude. It begins with the knowledge that Saúl Zuratas is a social outcast. He is Jewish, a member of an outcast community "pariah among the world's societies" (Vargas Llosa 1989a: 243). But he is even marginal as a Jew because he was never fully accepted in the Jewish community of Lima, and he had "given up believing in God" (Vargas Llosa 1989a: 9). Furthermore, he was born with a disfiguring birthmark on his face, making him "a marginal among marginals" (Vargas Llosa 1989a: 243):

> Saúl Zuratas had a dark birthmark, the color of wine dregs, that covered the entire right side of his face... The birthmark spared neither his ears nor his lips nor his nose, also puffy and misshapen from swollen veins. He was the ugliest lad in the world... (Vargas Llosa 1989: 8)[18]

Apparently, Zuratas fled modern society to join the Machiguengas and become "dissolved in a collective being" (Vargas Llosa 1989a: 243) where his birthmark would not separate him from others the way it had in his life up to that point. The Machiguengas accepted him, and eventually he became an *hablador*, which is cause for doubt in the mind of the author/narrator of the odd-numbered sections.

> Becoming a storyteller was adding what appeared impossible to what was merely improbable... Talking the way a storyteller talks means being able to feel and live in the very heart of that culture, means having penetrated its essence, reached the marrow of its history and mythology, given body to its taboos, images, ancestral desires, and terrors. It means being, in the most profound way possible, a rooted Machiguenga, one of that ancient lineage who... roamed the forests of my country, bringing and bearing away those tales, lies, fictions, gossip, and jokes that make a community of that people of scattered beings, keeping alive among them the feeling of oneness, of constituting something fraternal and solid. (Vargas Llosa 1989a: 244)[19]

In fact, Saúl Zuratas does not live up to this image. Though he is accepted into Machiguenga society, he is not content. Readers learn that he is not entirely faithful to Machiguenga culture. For example, his "stories continually display odd, off-centered women who do not fit any tribal behavioral pattern... these examples of difference are meant to open up the tribe to new ways of perceiving women" (Acosta Cruz: 140). The key word here is "difference." In his quest to have Machiguengas treat women better, Zuratas is dividing individuals from the whole "oneness" and "sameness" of Machiguenga society.

Machiguenga society is described as a model of pre-modern wholeness. Divisions in the society do not exist. Even the basic division between men an women is really more of a division between men and property (hence Zuratas' attempts to change the status of women). The Machiguengas have no individual names for different members of the tribe. The men are all called Tasurinchi and the women only described as the wife of Tasurinchi (i.e. 'wife' in a collective sense). Most importantly, the Machiguenga custom of physical purity, enforced by infanticide, assures that physical perfection will keep the tribe's homogeneity relatively intact. This custom's "naturalness" or appropriateness for a pre-modern native culture is reinforced by the revelation that wild animals generally kill their young when they are born different.

But Zuratas challenges the custom of physical purity. He rescues a baby parrot, born with a physical deformity, before it is killed by its mother and makes it into his companion "totem" parrot (Vargas Llosa 1989a: 232-234). Significantly, the bird is given his own nickname from Lima: Mascarita. In his last narrative, Zuratas the *hablador* challenges the custom directly and is put off:

> When the hablador intervenes through intertextuality to change the tribal custom of infanticide, his narrative reports that the audience laugh and then get angry. *Calma, calma, no se enojen. ¿De qué gritan?* (200)[20] The reaction of the audience is important here because they resist his intervention... Here their reactions show the Indians as active (and somewhat hostile) participants. (Acosta Cruz: 141)

Zuratas' efforts to change the practice stem from his knowledge that it would certainly have resulted in his own killing at birth had he been born Machiguenga.

What Zuratas fails to realize is that by introducing such concepts as women's rights (or any kind of rights) and the acceptance of physical differences, he is interposing modern individuality into a culture based on wholeness and unity. He is, in fact, opening the door to modern solitude. The paradox is that Saúl Zuratas fled modern society to be in a society where individual difference was eliminated by an overwhelming wholeness, yet he is not "one" with the Machiguengas either. This modern man is forever marginal, unhappy with difference he is also not satisfied with oneness. Reason keeps him solitary because it follows him wherever he goes.

Perhaps the most telling portrait of solitude given in the works of Mario Vargas Llosa is his critique of the Latin American code of *hombría*. To understand this critique, it is necessary to return briefly to Octavio Paz.

The code of *hombría* begins, for Paz, with the basic attitude of the male in Latin American society (Paz speaks of "the Mexican" macho, of course):

> The Mexican lives life as combat. This attitude does not make him any different from anyone else in the modern world. For other people, however, the manly ideal consists in an open and aggressive fondness for combat, whereas we emphasize defensiveness, the readiness to repel any attack. The Mexican *macho*—the male—is a hermetic being, closed up in himself, capable of guarding both himself and whatever has been confided to him. Manliness is judged according to one's invulnerability to enemy arms or the impacts of the outside world. (Paz 1985: 31) [21]

Defensiveness is the key to this way of dealing with the world. The *macho* is closed to all attempts to penetrate his being. Once this is understood, the significance of the verb *chingar* in Mexico leads to a better understanding of the *macho* and the code of *hombría*:

> The verb [*chingar*] denotes violence, an emergence from oneself to penetrate another by force. It also means to injure, to lacerate, to violate—bodies, souls, objects—and to destroy...
>   The idea of breaking, of ripping open, appears in a great many of these expressions. The word has sexual connotations but it is not

a synonym for the sexual act: one may *chingar* a woman without actually possessing her. And when it does allude to the sexual act, violation or deception gives it a particular shading. The man who commits it never does so with the consent of the chingada...

The person who suffers this action is passive, inert and open, in contrast to the active, aggressive and closed person who inflicts it. The *chingón* is the macho, the male; he rips open the *chingada*, the female, who is pure passivity, defenseless against the exterior world. The relationship between them is violent, and it is determined by the cynical power of the first and the impotence of the second. The idea of violence rules darkly over all the meanings of the word... (Paz 1985: 76-77)[22]

For Paz, "the *macho* is the *gran chingón*..." This one word communicates the essence of the code of *hombría*, "it is force without the discipline of any notion of order: arbitrary power, the will without reins and without a set course" (Paz 1985: 81). The person who is invulnerable, powerful, closed, is the master of *hombría*; the person who is vulnerable, weak, open, is the victim of the code of *hombría*.[23]

In the works of Mario Vargas Llosa, Peruvian society and all relations between men and women are governed by the code of *hombría*. "Fictional characters in Vargas Llosa's works are first isolated in a particular caste or class, by color or geographic origin, and second, within their caste, by the mask of *hombría* that each is expected to wear" (Feustle: 524-525).

In Vargas Llosa's *The Time of the Hero*, *hombría* is the code that governs the lives of the cadets at the Leoncio Prado military academy. Cadets compete with each other to establish an order based on the ability of the *chingón* to violate others.

The Leoncio Prado is the location for all manner of sexual activity—bestiality (a chicken and a dog), homosexual rape of a younger and weaker student, group masturbation... Each of these episodes has... a common denominator: they are expressions of *hombría*. Through these acts, the macho shows his peers that he is indeed capable of sex with animals, of imposing himself on another male, or of ejaculating first. He is *macho* because he is capable of *violating* another body. (Feustle: 527)

The element of violence associated with the code of *hombría* is clear in all of Vargas Llosa's works. It is often associated with the sex act:

> Sex does not exculpate but rather serves to sharpen the complexes of social inferiority, containing "a dose of humiliation for the one" and leaving the other with a "clear conscience"... There is no "humiliation" for Ambrosio because he is the active agent; he penetrates, violates the other... Likewise, there is no humiliation for the young men of the Leoncio Prado who have intercourse with animals and other cadets for the same reason: through these acts they are violating, expressing their *hombría*. (Feustle: 527)

The social consequences of following the code of *hombría* are evident throughout the novel. The most obvious symbol for the barbaric nature of the code is the fact that most of the cadets are known by their animal nicknames: "Jaguar," "Boa," "Piraña," "Gallo," etc. "This is more than just an animal label, however, as the characters are described as physically resembling the creatures. What is more, the behavior, activities, and general condition of the characters are clearly likened to those of more primitive beings" (Hancock: 38). Early in the novel, Alberto Fernández ("The Poet") has nightmares that clearly suggest that the code of *hombría* is really the law of the jungle. Even the image of the labyrinth is present:

> "I think I'm sick, Lieutenant. I mean mentally, not physically. I have nightmares every night." Alberto had lowered his eyes, feigning humility, and he spoke very slowly, his mind a blank, letting his lips and tongue talk on by themselves, letting them weave a spider web, a labyrinth. "They're awful, Lieutenant. Sometimes I dream I'm a killer, or sometimes these animals with human faces are chasing me. I wake up sweating and shaking. It's horrible, Lieutenant, honest." (Vargas Llosa 1966a: 17)[24]

By the end of the novel, a series of events involving three cadets in particular—The Jaguar, Ricardo Arana ("the Slave"), and Alberto Fernández ("the Poet")—has occurred that forces the reader to make ethical evaluations of their conduct and, implicitly, the code of *hombría*. The Jaguar is Vargas Llosa's example of the *gran chingón*. He proves himself "more of a man" than other cadets because he never cracks:

> He remains closed and is always the one who "opens," never leaving himself "open." Opposite to Jaguar is the "Slave," Ricardo Arana, the one student who is "open" and who pays for it with his

life...   Alberto Fernández is a character situated between the
extremes that Jaguar and the "Slave" represent. (Feustle: 525)

In the novel, Arana "the Slave" is killed during combat exercises
and readers learn that the Jaguar is probably responsible. Arana had
turned in another student for stealing an exam, breaking the code and
leading to his murder for revenge. Fernández "the Poet" names the
Jaguar as murderer but is rebuffed by school authorities who are anxious
to have the killing remain an "accident" in the eyes of the world. Jaguar
learns about the Poet's breach of "the code," but does not take revenge
because he is falsely blamed (and ostracized) by the other cadets in the
section for a general shakedown provoked by the Poet's accusations.
His changed motives are a dramatic condemnation of the code of
hombría from the *gran chingón* himself:

> All along Jaguar believes that Arana was wrong to squeal on Cava
> in order to get a pass. In the final moments of the novel, the two
> strong men, Lieutenant Gamboa and Jaguar—both of whom
> represent outwardly different but inwardly similar codes of
> honor—meet before going their separate ways. Jaguar, rejecting the
> code, admits his error but becomes its victim when the other cadets
> decide that he has turned informer on them, causing a shakedown
> and general punishment for everyone. Their mistake infuriates him,
> and he sees them as traitors. Jaguar is unable to reveal that it was
> Alberto who had turned informer because his reasons for betraying
> Jaguar were different—more noble—than the other cadets' betrayal
> of Jaguar's leadership. When Gamboa asks Jaguar why he does not
> tell the cadets that Alberto was to blame, Jaguar becomes very
> disturbed: "'But his case is different,' he said hoarsely, forcing out
> the words. 'It isn't the same at all, Sir. The others betrayed me out
> of plain cowardice. He [Alberto] wanted revenge for the Slave.
> He's a squealer and that's the worst thing you can be, but he did it to
> get revenge for a friend. Don't you see the difference, Sir?'" (385).
> (Gerdes: 44-45)

The novel's epilogue makes some surprising revelations. Both of
the novel's "strong men"—Lieutenant Gamboa (an archetype of the pure
and honorable soldier) and the Jaguar—reject their codes of honor.
Gamboa, recognizing the military's complicity in refusing to accept the
facts about Arana's killing, rejects the Jaguar's confession. The Jaguar,
in attempting to confess in order to save Gamboa from reassignment to a

remote Andean outpost, opens himself to justice—a clear violation of the code of *hombría*.

The fate of Alberto Fernández is disturbing. Unlike the Jaguar, he capitulates to the code of *hombría* by returning to civilian life and adopting the lifestyle of his father, an upper class "Don Juan" whose whole life is built around the social structure created by the code of *hombría*. This turn of events is especially disappointing for two reasons: first, because Alberto repeatedly condemns his father's lifestyle on the basis of how much it hurts his mother (the *chingón-chingada* relationship is obvious here); and second, because throughout the novel, the Poet/Fernández is presented as the character most accessible to the reader's sympathy.

Surprisingly, the Jaguar's story is different. At the end of the novel he marries his high school sweetheart and takes a job as a bank clerk but only after recognizing his past guilt, grieving for it, and *opening himself up* to his sweetheart by telling her everything about his past life. During the course of the novel, all three of the main characters date a girl named Teresa (Teresita, Teresa, Tere), but only the Jaguar ends up together with this girl at the end of the novel. Only the Jaguar is able to move beyond the solitude of the code of *hombría* and into the arms of love.

LOVE

The Jaguar finds an escape from the code of *hombría* in his love for Tere. Love lifts him out of himself and makes him content to remain outside of the struggle for power and status. This is a message that appears over and over again in the works of Paz, Vargas Llosa and García Márquez. Love is presented as something that can lift one out of one's self in modernity and achieve some kind of higher communion. It is recognized as an antidote for solitude.

Mario Vargas Llosa's novels generally present bleak pictures of Peruvian (and Latin American) society, but where some breach of modern solitude is presented, it usually depends on the love that connects two characters. The Jaguar at the end of *The Time of the Hero* is an excellent example. The love of Anselmo and Antonia in *The Green House* is also of this character. Even the impoverished lifestyle pursued by Santiago Zavala (*Conversation in the Cathedral*) with his wife Ana is an escape from (and implicit challenge to) the modern solitude caused by Peruvian social stratification and the code of *hombría.*   Though it may not seem appropriate to North American readers, even the brothels so frequently encountered in Vargas Llosa's novels are symbols of this kind of escape from solitude:

> The brothel was the temple of that clandestine religion, where one went to celebrate an exciting and perilous rite, to live, for a few short hours, a life apart. A life founded on terrible social injustices, no doubt... but the truth is that it gave many of us a very intense, respectful, and almost mystical relationship to the world and the practices of sex, something inseparable from the intuition of the sacred and of ceremony, of the active unfolding of fantasy, of mystery and shame, of everything that Georges Bataille calls transgression. (Vargas Llosa 1994: 188-189)

The "sacred" experience that Vargas Llosa refers to in this statement is directly related to the kind of mystical experience of communion that Octavio Paz associates with the fiestas and rituals of Mexican life.   For Paz, these ceremonies are events in which the Mexican "opens out" [*se abre al exterior*] and "discharges his soul" (Paz 1985: 49) [*Descarga su alma* (Paz 1959: 43)].   They are "the brilliant reverse to our silence and apathy, our reticence and gloom" (Paz 1985: 49) [*el revés brillante de nuestro silencio y apatía, de nuestra reserva y hosquedad* (Paz 1959: 44)].   In Paz's rituals and Vargas Llosa's brothels, solitude is swept away for a brief time and the absolute present restored. The base of this experience is always, if not love, then at least communion.   It is a kind of communication that opens up the isolated self to others and sweeps away solitude.

> Myths and fiestas, whether secular or religious, permit man to emerge from his solitude and become one with creation. therefore myth—disguised, obscure, hidden—reappears in almost all our acts and intervenes decisively in our history: it opens the doors of communion. (Paz 1985: 211)[25]

Nevertheless, such myths (rituals) and fiestas, and especially Vargas Llosa's brothels, are only an approximation of the communion that can be opened up by love between two people.   For both Paz and Vargas Llosa, the modern environment surrounding both the fiesta and the brothel prevent them from being more than a temporary escape from solitude:

> Vargas Llosa has reiterated the use of the house of prostitution as a metaphor for the difficulty of attaining love in the society of his novels. Although Antonia and Anselmo inhabit a magical precinct within the Casa Verde, their love in inevitably compromised by the love bought and sold in the surrounding milieu. The death of Antonia functions as a scapegoat's in that it absolves and epiphanizes her love for Anselmo; she dies because she has loved in a manner and a place unacceptable to society. (M. Davis: 537)

Love itself is thus an even greater break with solitude than either brothels or fiestas can provide. "Love abolishes solitude, self-centeredness, the individual, and ushers in the experience of wholeness through the communion of two opposites (man and woman), a metaphor of the liberation of the individual into a collectivity" (Wilson: 55). Love transgresses all established bounds in society, and thus...

> Love... is an antisocial act... Whenever it succeeds in realizing itself, it breaks up a marriage and transforms it into what society does not want it to be: a revelation of two solitary beings who create their own world, a world that rejects society's lies, abolishes time and work, and declares itself to be self-sufficient. (Paz 1985: 199-200) [26]

Gabriel García Márquez's most important study of love is presented in his novel *Love in the Time of Cholera* (1988).[27] In this book, he illustrates an understanding of love that is both similar to Paz's perception of love and different from it. García Márquez uses his characters to push love beyond the present moment to a more fully mature, wholesome perception of love characteristic of the autumn of life. This kind of love is important because it both retains the experience of communion so critical to Paz and at the same time suggests the possibility of something more.

The novel begins with the death of Jeremiah de Saint-Amour, by suicide, at the age of sixty years. Jeremiah is described as a cripple, without the use of his legs, but also as an "aesthetic saint" who "loved life with a senseless passion" (García Márquez 1988: 15). He is an important character in the text even though the reader never encounters him alive (save in someone else's memory) for he is a symbol for passionate, earthly love.

Jeremiah de Saint-Amour loves life passionately, but he does not love deeply. He knows that he will not be able to survive into old age, just as passionate, earthly love cannot survive the rigors of old age. In the prime of his life he declares that he will never grow old:

> A long time ago, on a deserted beach in Haiti where the two of them lay naked after love, Jeremiah de Saint-Amour had sighed: "I will never be old." She [his lover] interpreted this as a heroic determination to struggle without quarter against the ravages of time, but he was more specific: he had made the irrevocable decision to take his own life when he was sixty years old. (García Márquez 1988: 15) [28]

Jeremiah de Saint-Amour is a deliberate, clear-headed and rational individual. It is in this respect that Dr. Juvenal Urbino is, as Jeremiah would say, "his soul's friend" [*un amigo del alma*], despite the fact that "the only affinity between the two was their addiction to chess understood as a dialogue of reason and not as a science" (García Márquez 1988: 15) [*la única afinidad de ambos era el vicio del ajedrez entendido como un diálogo de la razón y no como una ciencia.* (García Márquez 1985: 25)]. Chess is itself an important symbol of Jeremiah's life. In his life as in his chess, he looks several moves ahead, and the unfinished game he abandons at the scene of his death is symbolic of his decision to abandon old age. He sees that he will be mated in four moves. Then, despite his reputation as an "indomitable soldier, accustomed to fighting to the last drop of blood," Jeremiah de Saint-Amour surrenders "without honor... as if his death had been not his own decision but an inexorable destiny" (García Márquez 1988: 7, 14, 15).

The life of this odd character may be interpreted not only as symbolic of the passionate love characteristic of youth and adulthood but also as the embodiment of Octavio Paz's philosophy of love. If love is confined to the kind of experience Paz describes, then no return to the "absolute present" is possible once the fires of human passion turn cool in the autumn of life. Jeremiah de Saint-Amour's disillusionment represents the despair of a man who knows that there will be no more climactic ecstasies to redeem his desolate existence, no more communion to transfigure his solitude, no more returns to the absolute present. Dr. Juvenal Urbino, who investigates the scene of the suicide, notes several times that it is unusual (and somehow sad) to find a suicide by gold cyanide fumes that is not for love. He does not understand that Jeremiah de Saint-Amour's death was for "unrequited love" after all; he despairs for the erotic love that does not return to the old.

García Márquez's novel begins with the death of tempestuous earthly love, which is no mistake since the novel leads in a different direction. He wants to suggest that there is a deeper kind of love, and that this quieter but more fully developed love can both achieve the experience of Paz's absolute present and go beyond it to reach outside the limited circle of two lovers. After Jeremiah de Saint-Amour's death, Dr. Urbino is upset that his friend deceived him for so long about his true identity. Passion, García Márquez is telling us, often masquerades as love, but it is really only a glimpse of how much greater love can be.

Urbino does not see until the moment of his own death (later the same day) that even his love for his wife is far deeper than the romance they shared in their life together. "Only God knows how much I loved you" (García Márquez 1988: 43), he says to his wife as he dies. His life's work is mirrored in the manner of his death, as he is killed in a fall while attempting to catch a colorful parrot, just as in life he has striven to capture the social image of happiness. Romantic love—society's image of love—really only brushes the surface of love the way that the parrot's speech brushes the surface of language. Juvenal Urbino knows this as he dies. "He looked at her for the last and final time with eyes more luminous, more grief-stricken, more grateful than she had ever seen them in half a century of a shared life..." (García Márquez 1988: 42). His sorrow is for dying without her, for he has not seen the truth in time to share it with her. Fermina Daza's revelation must wait for her own moment of discovery.

After her husband's death, Fermina must recover her identity in order to discover the true depth of her own love.

> She wanted to be herself again, to recover all that she had been obliged to give up in half a century of servitude that had doubtless made her happy but which, once her husband was dead, did not leave her even the vestiges of her identity. She was a ghost in a strange house that overnight had become immense and solitary and through which she wandered without purpose, asking herself which of them was deader: the man who had died or the woman he had left behind. (García Márquez 1988: 279) [29]

There is no doubt that the marriage of Dr. Juvenal Urbino and Fermina Daza was a happy one. Fermina never regretted having married the young Dr. Urbino, and from the time of his death "she had no peace, but was careful about any gesture that might seem to betray her grief" (García Márquez 1988: 47). Nevertheless, like most marriages theirs was cluttered with the flotsam and jetsam of daily life, and Fermina must break out of that circle.

> The importance of her new status as widow is that now she can love Urbino in her own way, for she is certain that he is present, "still alive, but without his male caprices or his patriarchal demands, without the draining necessity for her to love him with the same ritual of inopportune kisses and tender words with which he loved her" (409). (McNerney: 86)

Fermina wonders, just as her husband did in his lifetime, about the depth of their love: "It is incredible how one can be happy for so many years in the midst of so many squabbles, so many problems, damn it, and not really know if it was love or not" (García Márquez 1988: 329). She will not discover how deep her love for her husband truly is until she breaks out of her marriage (and social) role at the end of the novel to pursue her own destiny.

She is afforded this opportunity by the strangest character in the entire novel, and its protagonist, Mr. Florentino Ariza. At the beginning of the novel and through most of its pages...

> Florentino is the personification of the most romantic notions of love; it rules his life. He not only promises to love forever, he does it. His actions and thoughts are always linked in some way to his love for Fermina Daza, and he is absolutely sure that no one on the face of the earth has as great a capacity for love as he does. (McNerney: 75)

At first accepted as a suitor to Fermina Daza in his youth, but then unceremoniously rejected, Florentino Ariza continues to love her from afar while pursuing his own destiny. As he matures, Florentino personifies the seasons of love, using passionate love as a way of helping him to forget for brief moments his love for Fermina Daza, until by the day of Dr. Juvenal Urbino's death he is earthly love aged to the edge of perfection, like a fine wine ready for the table.

The date of his achievement is significant. It is the same day that witnesses the deaths of both Jeremiah de Saint-Amour and Dr. Juvenal Urbino: Pentecost Sunday.   In the Christian Church, Pentecost celebrates the anniversary of the coming of the Holy Spirit, the day when Christ's disciples were filled with the Holy Spirit and charged with spreading the Gospel (good news) to other lands and peoples.   In the context of the novel, the fact that all of these events come together on Pentecost Sunday represents the passing of youthful, erotic love (the suicide of Jeremiah de Saint-Amour) and the coming of the spirit of mature love (to Juvenal Urbino at his death, and to Florentino Ariza). Florentino's renewed calling to pursue his love for Fermina Daza and spread the (holy) spirit of love that has come to him is also encompassed by the image of Pentecost.

Like the angel of that spirit of love he represents, Florentino renews his lover's suit.   At first he is rebuffed, but his patient maturity eventually draws Fermina out and sets her on the path to her own discovery of love.

Fermina Daza's final spiritual journey (together with Florentino Ariza's) is represented by the voyage of the riverboat "New Fidelity" [*Nueva Fidelidad*] at the end of the novel.   After a long courtship compressed into only a few days time, the two make an attempt at passionate love.   As if to confirm their distance from such eroticism, the attempt at first fails completely and then proves unsatisfactory.   "They did not try to make love again until much later, when the inspiration came to them without their looking for it.   They were satisfied with the simple joy of being together" (García Márquez 1988: 341).   When they do make love again, it is "the tranquil, wholesome love of experienced grandparents" (García Márquez 1988: 345).

> It was as if they had leapt over the arduous calvary of conjugal life and gone straight to the heart of love.   They were together in silence like an old married couple wary of life, beyond the pitfalls of passion, beyond the brutal mockery of hope and the phantoms of disillusion: beyond love.   For they had lived together long enough to know that love was always love, anytime and anyplace, but it was more solid [*denso*] the closer it came to death.   (García Márquez 1988: 345)[30]

This last insight is the kingpin.   The knowledge of impending death makes love more "*denso*" (more dense, more thick, more close), more tangibly real than ever. The image of José Ortega y Gasset's "shipwreck" is never clearer. Florentino Ariza recalls once that love becomes greater and nobler in calamity. The calamity of approaching death is equivalent to the calamity of Ortega y Gasset's shipwreck; it is what makes the effort to swim—to love—so essential.

That García Márquez believes his vision of mature love to be the equivalent of Paz's passionate moment of "absolute time" and the experience of "communion" is made clear in the conclusion of *Love in the Time of Cholera*, where Florentino and Fermina end their story sailing "forever" in an infinite circle up and down the river of love.

LOVE AS LIFESTYLE

> *the two took off their clothes and made love*
> *to protect our share of all that's eternal,*
> *to defend our ration of paradise and time,*
> *to touch our roots, to rescue ourselves,*
> *to rescue the inheritance stolen from us*
> *by the thieves of life centuries ago,*
> *the two took off their clothes and kissed*
> *because two bodies, naked and entwined,*
> *leap over time, they are invulnerable,*
> *nothing can touch them, they return to the source,*
> *there is no you, no I, no tomorrow,*
> *no yesterday, no names, the truth of two*
> *in a single body, a single soul,*
> *oh total being...*
>
> —"Sunstone" (Paz 1987: 19)

Love, says Paz, is the key to leaping over the time of modernity. Solitude is dissolved in the act of love and the lovers return to the "source," beyond the reach of time and mundane reality. But can love be turned into a lifestyle?

In Latin America, as elsewhere, solitude is one of the chief consequences of the characteristic trends of modernity. Individual "selves" are separated from the community and isolated in their jobs, in their families, in their churches, even in their pastimes. The self is divided to such an extent that it no longer has one shape but many masks, each appropriate to its own forum but incompatible with the others. The things of the modern world too are monotonously solitary.

One hotel room is cloned a billion times and appears everywhere. London, Lima, Mexico City, Phoenix: all are cities of mirrors like the one dreamed by José Arcadio Buendía, endlessly repeating the same forms and patterns. The cultural problem of modernity is present everywhere and for the most part the same.

There are two aspects of modern solitude (and the cultural problem of modernity) that seem more pronounced in Latin America than elsewhere, however. Both of these aspects stem from what has been called the "original sin" of Latin America. "The original sin of Latin America was the sin of rape—the rape of native civilizations and of the native women by the conquerors" (Feustle: 523). The divisions between people created by such factors as race and the code of *hombría* are towering barriers in Latin America where they do not seem as important elsewhere. Their presence may be interpreted as either a holdover from the past or a division that modernity exacerbates. Evidence exists to support both views. Either way, they are clearly important aspects of the Latin American experience of modernity and deserve more study within the theoretical framework of modernity.

Love is the antithesis of *hombría*, racism, class divisions, and all the aspects of modern rationalism that tend to separate and silence individual persons. When asked where the solitude of the Buendías comes from, García Márquez replied

> From their lack of love, I think. You can see in the book that in a whole century the Aureliano with the pig's tale is the only Buendía to have been conceived with love. The Buendías were incapable of loving and this is the key to their solitude and their frustration. (Mendoza and García Márquez: 75)

Are modern people also incapable of loving? Much of what has been written on modernity in Europe is either silent on this subject or else skeptical of "love's" potential.

Gabriel García Márquez, for one, seems to hold out more hope for relying on love as a way to penetrate the cultural problem of modernity. His unique look at mature love takes what is best about Paz's vision of passionate love, including its potential for overcoming solitude, and enriches it to the point that it could become the basis for a new way of coming to grips with modernity. Of course, love will never conquer modernity, but García Márquez never implies that it will, or even that it should. At most, love in the mature sense that he explores in *Love in the*

Time of Cholera will be a new swimming stroke: a better way to tread water, in the sense of José Ortega y Gasset's image of the shipwreck of modern life.

The mature "love" of Florentino Ariza and Fermina Daza, and even of Juvenal Urbino as he dies, is a love that incorporates the circular renewal of Paz's absolute present within its own compass. Shakespeare is also said to have done something very similar in his later years when he abandoned both comedy and tragedy to create his "romances": plays which are whole creations in the sense that they are both comic and tragic, and contain circular patterns that return to spiritual and physical renewal by the closing scene. In some ways, Vargas Llosa's admiration for the "total novel," which he explores in great detail in *The Perpetual Orgy* (1986a),[31] also bears a resemblance to this circular structure which seeks to encompass both separateness and solidarity, solitude and love.

In the end, Paz argues, the problem with modern solitude is that it does not encompass any opposite; it is never redeemed by love. Thus it is "sterile." But can the transfiguring effect of love as envisioned by either Paz or García Márquez be achieved at a collective level? For both Paz and Ortega y Gasset, this is the "theme of our times" (Paz 1985: 212). Its possibilities are explored in the next chapter.

---

1. For the original Spanish text, see Paz, 1959, page 175.
2. The words are taken from Peter Shaffer's *Equus*: "The Normal is the good smile in a child's eyes: — alright. It is also the dead stare in a million adults. It both sustains and kills — like a god. It is the Ordinary made beautiful: it is also the Average made lethal. The Normal is the indispensable, murderous God of Health..." (Shaffer: 56)
3. For the original Spanish text, see Paz, 1990, pages 44-45.
4. For the original Spanish text, see Paz, 1959, page 184.
5. For the original Spanish text, see Paz, 1950a, pages 57-58.
6. For the original Spanish text, see García Márquez, 1975, page 187.
7. The Colonel also appears as the central character—though unnamed—in *No One Writes to the Colonel* (1968) and is mentioned in *Leaf Storm* (1972).
8. For the original Spanish text, see García Márquez, 1967, page 113.
9. Wood calls it "an inability to mourn, abetted perhaps by a strangled

regret, the belated, self-protecting thought that it would have been better to have felt nothing at all. (Wood: 97)

10. For the original Spanish text, see García Márquez, 1967, page 192.

11. For the original Spanish text, see García Márquez, 1967, pages 211-212.

12. *Pantaleón y las visitadoras* (1973); *El hablador* (1987); and *La ciudad y los perros* (1965).

13. The theme of "organization" itself makes for an interesting study. For more on this approach, see Williams (1978).

14. For the original Spanish text, see Vargas Llosa, 1973, page 70.

15. For the original Spanish text, see Vargas Llosa, 1993a, pages 191-192.

16. For the original Spanish text, see Vargas Llosa, 1993, pages 11-12.

17. *La tía Julia y el escribidor* (1977).

18. For the original Spanish text, see Vargas Llosa, 1987, page 11.

19. For the original Spanish text, see Vargas Llosa, 1987, pages 233-234.

20. "Don't get excited, don't get angry. Wherefore do you shout?" (my translation).

21. For the original Spanish text, see Paz, 1959, page 19.

22. For the original Spanish text, see Paz, 1959, pages 69-70.

23. Gabriel García Márquez defines *machismo* (*hombría* by a different name) as "merely the usurpation of other people's rights" (Mendoza and García Márquez: 108). This definition is consistent with Paz's.

24. For the original Spanish text, see Vargas Llosa, 1965, page 19.

25. For the original Spanish text, see Paz, 1959, page 190.

26. For the original Spanish text, see Paz, 1959, page 179.

27. *El amor en los tiempos del cólera* (1985).

28. For the original Spanish text, see García Márquez, 1985, page 26.

29. For the original Spanish text, see García Márquez, 1985, page 381.

30. For the original Spanish text, see García Márquez, 1985, pages 469-470.

31. *La orgía perpetua* (1975a).

CHAPTER 7

Power, Politics, and Recovery

> *The only effective weapon against orthodoxies is criticism; in order to defend ourselves against intolerance and fanaticisms we have no other recourse than to exercise, firmly but with lucidity, the opposing virtues: tolerance and freedom of spirit.*[1]
>
> Octavio Paz (1978: 458)
> *Mexico and the United States*
> [my translation]

> *Love and politics are two poles linked by an arch: the person.*
> Octavio Paz (1999: 16)
> *Itinerary*

In the first part of this study, the political problem of modernity was shown to be an outgrowth of the cultural and philosophical problems of modernity. It is the stifling atmosphere of cultural modernity—the modernity of the triumph of system (the iron cage of capitalism and bureaucracy) over self—that stifles the deliberative ideals of equality and democracy. In Latin American literature this condition (the condition of the isolated and divided self) is often represented as solitude, and its solution as some kind of "communion" or return to an unbroken fellowship. The political problem of modernity then is the same problem in both Europe and Latin America: how can modern men and women reinvigorate the deliberative ideals of the enlightenment within the prevailing conditions of modernity?

One "solution" that has been put forward many times in both theory and practice is enforced modernization. Here, democracy and equality are set aside completely while the economic and administrative institutions of modernity are created. In theory, this is a necessary evil designed to impart the blessings of "stability" on such institutions so that they will be able to withstand the immense pressures characteristic of "open" societies. It is a subtle argument.[2]

But the reality of enforced modernization is not so subtle. Enforced modernization today amounts to a reprise of Peter the Great's violent inversion of backward Russia. As St. Petersburg's experience makes clear and as the failed programs of many Latin American dictators and juntas also show, enforced modernization—even at its best—leads only to the spectral world of the modernism of underdevelopment. When political backwardness is engineered and administered by the state the correct image is not that of a concerned midwife eager to assist in the birth of a new order, but rather one of the aging courtier determined to maintain his old influence with new methods designed for a changed environment. It is the old autocracy hidden behind a modern economic facade.

The Critique of Power in Latin American literature is aimed directly at the modernization of underdevelopment. Power in the service of "development" without democracy is not only the negation of modernity, it is the reassertion of the authority of absolutes in history. This reactionary pressure, which extends both to the forms that domination can take and to ideology, is in fact none other than the age-old problem of power. The modern disguises of this old devil, as comprehended by Octavio Paz, Gabriel García Márquez, and Mario Vargas Llosa, will be explored in the first part of this chapter.

The second part of the chapter returns to a more positive theme. Can the deliberative values of the Enlightenment, equality and democracy, be restored amid the conditions of modernity? There are no obvious answers, though all of the authors encountered in this study demonstrate—in either their words or their actions (or both)—that they believe there is at least some room for hope. Perhaps more importantly, they have all engaged in the practice, as José Ortega y Gasset did, of cultural criticism. Shipwreck may be the fundamental condition of human life, but neither Paz, nor García Márquez, nor Vargas Llosa is yet ready to yield before the storm. Indeed, the storm may be where they, and humanity at its best, are most at home.

POWER

Octavio Paz's condemnation of the Latin American code of *hombría* and the solitude it creates has already been discussed, but for Paz the excessive *machismo* of Latin societies is only a single manifestation of the much greater underlying problem of power. The nature of this problem is evident in the code of *hombría* and the character of the *chingón* but not limited to such phenomena. For Paz, the problem of power is evident wherever "absolutes" of any kind are used to dominate or control individual human beings.

"Absolutes," in this sense, can take on many forms. Besides the code of *hombría* and the actions of the *chingón*, Paz also cites such examples as the Latin American figure of the "*caudillo*" (or strong man), a highly intolerant religious tradition (based on the importance of the counter-reformation in Spanish history), and, most importantly, the infectious lure of absolutist ideologies.

The reason such absolutes are abhorrent to Paz is simple: they dehumanize people. In order for an absolute

> ...to realize itself as a totality it must define itself in terms of what opposes it. Thus the *other* comes into being. This *other* is not merely the political adversary who professes opinions that are different from ours: he is the enemy of the absolute, the absolute enemy. He must be exterminated [Paz's emphasis]. (Paz 1985a: 182)[3]

Thus the very presence of an absolute whether in political forms or in ideology implies the destruction of some kind of opposition. But if absolutisms imply the elimination of all "others" (in Paz's sense) then they also must imply the absence of democracy or any kind of free politics, because where there is no respect for difference, there can be no peaceful coexistence between free individuals.

Caudillismo has its roots, according to Paz, as far back as the Moorish occupation of Spain which lasted several centuries. The rule of Islam (and its overthrow in the sixteenth century) affected Spanish culture in many ways (some positive, others less so) but its consequences are unmistakable:

> The fusion between the religious and the political, for example, or the notion of a crusade, appears in Hispanic attitudes with a more intense and more vivid coloration than is the case with the other European peoples. It is not an exaggeration to see in these traits the traces of Islam and its vision of the world and of history. (Paz 1985a: 161)[4]

One of the cultural traits that Islam left behind was its traditional social structure based around the leadership of a local strong man, a sheik or *sharif*. This tradition was brought to the new world in the conquistadors and their henchmen, persisted through Spanish rule and the *latifundio* and *hacienda* system, until by the time of the struggles between liberals and conservatives in the wars for independence the fact of *caudillo* rule was strong enough to repeatedly frustrate constitutional attempts to create democracy.[5]

The result of this manifestation of the problem of power has been two-fold. First, in countries such as Mexico, it has instituted a kind of cultural duplicity between the written constitutional rules about political power and the true sources and methods for using power in those states. In Paz's Mexico, for example, democratic forms exist, but true power is clearly in the hands of the Mexican president (whose most meaningful limitation is merely the prohibition against reelection to office). Second, in countries such a Cuba where a revolutionary Marxist government rules, *caudillismo* is itself the rule of the day and even the illusion of political rights and freedoms disappears. The fact that Castro's legitimacy is based to a great extent on this part of the Latin tradition is cause for great concern to Paz. "None of our dictators, not even the most brazen of them, has ever denied the historical legitimacy of democracy. The first regime to have dared to proclaim a different sort of legitimacy [in Latin America] was Castro's" (Paz 1985a: 176). Castro's claim to legitimacy is the claim of a *caudillo*, and it threatens the very idea of democracy in Latin America.

The problem of power is also present in Latin America's highly intolerant and absolutist religious tradition. According to Paz, the most important source of this trait was the Counter-Reformation in Spain. Shortly after the Reformation and the Renaissance...

Spain and Portugal closed themselves off and, retreating within
themselves, rejected the modernity that was dawning. The most
complete, radical and coherent expression of this rejection was the
Counter-Reformation. The Spanish monarchy identified itself with
a universal faith and with a unique interpretation of that faith...
Thus whereas the other European States tended more and more to
represent nationhood and to defend its particular values, the Spanish
State confused its cause with the cause of an ideology... The idea
of the universal mission of the Spanish people, defender of a
doctrine that was just and true, was a survival from medieval times
and Arabic culture which, grafted onto the body of the Spanish
monarchy, breathed new life into it in the beginning but eventually
paralyzed it. (Paz 1985a: 162)[6]

Like all absolutist ideologies, that of the church of the
Counter-Reformation damned all opposing belief systems at the same
moment that it claimed absolute supremacy for itself. In so doing, it
was swept up in the problem of power; it became isolated, ingrown,
solitary, and responsible for a litany of unspeakable crimes against
humanity. In other words, it became what it most opposed: a damnable
heresy. In excommunicating its "*others*," the absolutist ideology of the
church became its own worst enemy—its own "*other*." This is the
paradox of absolute power. Its very existence dehumanizes others, but
also at the same time and in the same act it dehumanizes itself.

The ideology that Paz most often criticizes in this way is Marxism
(though he does not look kindly on any form of absolutism). He is clear
about Marxism's nature as an ideology and not a science:

Marxism is not a body of knowledge or a method or investigation
but an ideology. It is so on two counts: in the Communist
countries, it hides social realities beneath a veil of concepts and thus
serves as a coverup for basically unjust social relations; and in the
non-Communist countries... it has turned into a "dogmatic
metaphysics." (Paz 1983: 176)[7]

As a "dogmatic metaphysics," Marxism does in the sphere of politics
just what Counter-Reformation Catholicism did in the sphere of
religion; it makes itself inhuman and reprehensible. Paz goes so far as
to call it "a lay version of a holy war" (Paz 1985a: 181).

Mario Vargas Llosa has, like Paz, seen the danger of absolutism in
ideological fanaticism. He has pointed out many times in interviews

that he thinks ideologies often take the place of reality in people's minds (especially those of intellectuals) and that this has a tendency to lead to violence (ICA Video: "Mario Vargas Llosa with John King"). "Intellectuals and artists have contributed in very important ways to the legitimization of violence as an instrument of change in Latin America" (Williams 1987: 205). Where ideology fosters certainty, Vargas Llosa suggests, violence often follows.

Vargas Llosa's most effective refutations of absolutist ideologies appear in *The Real Life of Alejandro Mayta* (1986), *The War of the End of the World* (1982), and *Death in the Andes* (1996).[8] In the first of these novels, Vargas Llosa creates the image of a would-be revolutionary hero and uses it to attack all forms of ideological crusaders. "Mayta, the ice cream man, represents not only the demythification of the revolutionary (Che Guevara, Fidel Castro, Sandino, Bolívar) but also the very denial of any such image" (Castro-Klarén: 205). As with other revolutionary ideologues, Mayta's plans for the new post-revolutionary society are less than sketchy; in fact, they don't exist. His whole project is built on revolutionary rhetoric attacking the current order.

> Mayta is unconvincing because his revolutionary project is never unfolded for the reader's consideration. It is a secret, a vague hope, a senseless crisscrossing of activities that seem unjustifiable. Mayta, in fact, never had a chance in real life, nor does he get a chance in this fictional pseudobiography... His final destiny is the only one he was suited for all along: ice cream man. (Castro-Klarén: 196)

No matter how persuasive an intellectual critique of the current order may be (as with the Marxist critique of capitalism), it cannot provide substantial guarantees for the success of alternative systems because by definition such systems do not yet exist. Indeed, as Vargas Llosa illustrates with Alejandro Mayta, revolutionary ideological projects (including Marxism) rarely bother to do much more than provide the vague outlines of some better time to come. In this way the persuasive critique of particulars often leads to an ideological world-view dominated by a kind of messianic absolutism. But pseudo-intellectual belief-systems like this can never justify killing one's fellow human beings for Vargas Llosa. So much for Alejandro Mayta, the political-intellectual revolutionary. Vargas Llosa sees a far more dangerous problem in the absolutism of the genuinely religious (or spiritual) revolutionary.

A more thorough investigation of the excesses and deceptions of absolutist ideologies is taken up in *The War of the End of the World*. The setting for this exhilarating novel is the backlands of Brazil at the time of the Canudos uprising in the 1890s.[9]   Its plot lines and rich nuances are too complicated to do them justice here, but all of the various narratives in this amazing novel take shape around the dramatic confrontation between the Brazilian military and a group of religious fanatics lead by an enigmatic character known as Antônio Conselheiro (Antônio the Counselor).   After four military expeditions are sent against Canudos by the Brazilian government, each one larger and better armed than the one before, the fanatics are finally defeated and Canudos is destroyed.

Ideology ranks high as a subject for investigation in this novel because of the numerous ideological positions that confront each other and because of the social blindness that they impose on their adherents. There are at least four ideologically-motivated groups competing in the novel: the traditional aristocracy (with monarchist tendencies), the middle-class republicans (who support the newly-established republic of Brazil), the Brazilian military (with its own ambitions), and the rebels in Canudos (who combine anti-republicanism with an odd communitarian and religious spirit).   The interesting thing is not so much that these different absolutist belief systems come into conflict with each other (nothing unusual in that) but that in so doing they create four completely different realities for the people living under their individual influences. Indeed, the rebel group at Canudos is, at least in the beginning if not throughout the entire novel, no threat in itself to any of the other three competing ideological factions, yet Canudos (or rather the reality that Canudos represents in the eyes of the other ideological positions) precipitates the entire conflict.

The rebels in Canudos, for example, view the newly established republican government of Brazil as the enemy of the church.   Their rhetoric equates it with the devil and the forces of hell.   Yet the Catholic Church itself eventually ends up condemning the odd sect that has formed in Canudos.   Indeed, the reader is left wondering whether the hated republican government would have bothered with Canudos at all if it didn't offer them an excuse for striking a blow against the traditional aristocracy.   At one point, a seizure of English weapons is staged by the republicans to implicate the aristocracy in some kind of monarchist conspiracy. When the military arrives at the scene in force, its members are convinced that they are going to war against "the English" and "freemasons," labels the rebels in Canudos would have found strange indeed. The rebels, by contrast, saw the soldiers as the forces of the anti-christ, something the poor foot soldiers, weary of the road and dreaming of home, would also have found unbelievable. Meanwhile, the traditional aristocracy, dumbfounded by the wonder of it all, sees the threat posed by the army and plots to work together with the republicans to minimize the military's influence.

By the end of the novel all four ideological factions have suffered tremendous defeats. Canudos has been destroyed and Antônio the counselor slain; the army is decimated; the traditional aristocracy weakened beyond recognition; the republican government humiliated—to say nothing of the multitude of smaller terrors that punctuate the lives of individual characters trying to work their way through this mess. By the time the atmosphere clears, the reader knows that all the pain and suffering in the novel was brought down for no other reason than because the absolutist ideologies of the competing factions demanded it. Vargas Llosa's point seems to be that nothing is worth the terrible suffering caused by dehumanization, especially not vague abstractions like ideologies.[10]

Perhaps Mario Vargas Llosa's most dismal commentary on the inhumanity of absolutism is found in his novel, *Death in the Andes*. Set in the fictional Andean mining town of Naccos, the entire novel is overshadowed by the omnipresent danger of surprise attack by Shining Path guerilla fighters. The rebels (or *terrucos*, as they are called in the novel) recognize no reality separate from their own ideology, and the political murders they commit in the novel illustrate how far from truth their reality can be. In one narrative, a pair of young French travelers are pulled off a bus and stoned to death by the side of the road, presumably for being foreign and thus somehow associated with global capitalism and the exploitation of Peru by foreigners.[11]   In another account, two agricultural scientists working on a project designed to benefit local Andean villagers are executed for being "people of privilege" and thus somehow also culpable under the rebels' strange ideological world view.[12]   Yet individual *terrucos* are not portrayed as monsters even in these inhuman scenes. They act as disciplined and responsible persons through even the worst violence, as if to underscore the ideologically-driven nature of their murders. In the few cases where readers are allowed to confront an individual rebel personality—such as

Asunta, the young woman *terruco* who is revealed to be the same girl who had been impregnated by the traveling merchant in an earlier narrative (Vargas Llosa 1996: 133-134)—the feeling left with the reader is not so much that of cringing in front of a trained killer or hardened sociopath as one of looking, astonished, up the barrel of a gun at one's own sister or an old friend. This, for Vargas Llosa the same as it was for Octavio Paz, is the terror of absolutism when it comes to dominate individual human beings.

But there are other dimensions of this kind of terror portrayed in *Death in the Andes* that are less explicitly ideological in nature. In fact, where the poet Octavio Paz begins with a conception of the problem of power as rooted in human nature and socio-cultural constructions (such as the code of *hombría* or the fusion of religious and political traditions) Vargas Llosa returns to a more visceral understanding of the problem of power only after having explored absolutism in its more intellectual, ideological forms. "*Death in the Andes* offers elements that point to an unprecedented turn in Vargas Llosa's fiction. For the first time the violent instincts of some characters no longer have any rational explanation whatsoever; violence just happens" (Kristal: 187). Absolutism, in its visceral Dionysian expression, incites people to violence without the reasoned excuses provided by ideology. Violence is no longer simply the instrument of those who exploit or the result of political fanaticism; it is something more fundamentally human that happens when people forget how to see their own humanity in the others around them.

> In *Death in the Andes*, some participate in the most depraved acts of murder and cannibalism for no apparent reason at all. The brutal massacre of the three people is therefore more disturbing and perverse than the killings of the Shining Path guerrillas, who justify violence as a means toward military and political aims, or the murder that Tomás Carreño commits when he thought his loved one was being tortured by the Hog. (Kristal: 195)

When the man referred to as "the blaster" confesses to participating in the ritual murder of the three missing persons in *Death in the Andes*, he cannot explain why he joined in the killings. Though he is tormented by the memory of the taste of the human organs he ate, he expresses no sense of guilt at having "communed" at the sacrifice. The experience of "oneness" that dominated "the blaster's" humanity during the ritual sacrifice is reminiscent of Octavio Paz' description of the eternal present recreated in the Mexican fiesta: it is the communion that realizes itself in the exclusion of others, the absolute that "defines itself in terms of what opposes it" (Paz 1985a: 182). In the end, the Dionysian communion in ritual is the same as the intellectual communion in ideology. Both are expressions of absolutism in human affairs. Both create "others" who are, in the same act of creation, deprived of their humanity and treated as mere objects to be manipulated or destroyed within the framework of some collective enterprise. Both are equally dehumanizing, equally limited in their understanding of the real conditions of life and equally bound-up in the problem of power.

Gabriel García Márquez' critique of power in The Autumn of the Patriarch (1976) has already been discussed. By the end of the novel, the Patriarch is depicted exactly as one might expect from Paz's and Vargas Llosa's depictions of the problem of absolutism inherent in any power position. The fact of the Patriarch's power separates him from all "others" and so dehumanizes his subjects. But in dehumanizing the "others" the Patriarch eventually ends up dehumanizing himself. The patriarch becomes what he has made other people in his realm—a mere object, devoid of humanity:

> The stronger the general grows, the more removed from humanity and truth he becomes... He often seems to be in limbo, marking time as he waits for an end that refuses to come. (De Feo: 59)

Finally, he is said to die as a solitary drowned man because of his lack of love.[13] (The allusion to José Ortega y Gasset is unmistakable.)

Another of García Márquez's books, *The General in His Labyrinth* (1990),[14] also takes the problem of power and absolutes as one of its most important themes, but this book reflects more accurately than García Márquez's earlier works not just the solitude of absolute power, but the solitude associated with the grand design of a visionary. As García Márquez depicts it, a grand vision can be life-affirming in itself, but the use of power to impose the vision always ends up dehumanizing both the master and his subjects.

The General in His Labyrinth focuses on the last few months in the life of the great liberator of Spanish America, Simón Bolívar. Bolívar's great dream for South America was to make it a single united federal state and so put it in a position to rival the power of North America and Europe. It is the hopelessness of this dream (or great visionary ideal) that leads to the general's depression as he sails down the Magdellena River to his deathbed at the plantation of San Pedro Alejandrino.

Bolívar's dream of Latin American unity is shared by García Márquez. At the end of his Nobel lecture in 1982, García Márquez says:

> We, the inventors of tales, who will believe anything, feel entitled to believe that it is not yet too late to engage in the creation of... a new and sweeping utopia of life, where no one will be able to decide for others how they die, where love will prove true and happiness be possible, and where the races condemned to one hundred years of solitude will have, at last and forever, a second opportunity on earth. (García Márquez 1988a: 90-91)

He is speaking not only of the Buendías in *One Hundred Years of Solitude*, but also of all Latin America. This is Bolívar's dream of unity. Though he is not a communist and does not share the communist version of a world united under Marxism, García Márquez's commitment to the unity of Latin America in some form is clear from his interviews:

> Are you a Communist?
>   Of course not. I am not and have never been. Nor have I belonged to any political party... As an anti-colonial Latin American, I take a position that annoys many interests in the United States... I am a Latin American, and considering all that is going on in Latin America, it would be a crime not to be interested in politics... The only choice I have is to be an emergency politician. (Playboy: 66-67)

It should not be surprising, since this dream of a united Latin America is shared by the author of *The General in His Labyrinth*,[15] that the solitude evident in García Márquez's depiction of Bolívar is somewhat ambiguous. The dehumanization of "others" caused by his absolute power is evident both in the events depicted in the novel and in Bolívar's personal deterioration (which may be seen as a consequence of his power). But the general's solitary decrepitude is mitigated by his grand vision of solidarity. Through his vision the general does know how to love. Perhaps it is a greater love than most others can comprehend.

Nothing pained or bewildered him more than people casting doubt
on his affections, and he was capable of parting oceans and moving
mountains with the terrible power of his charm until he convinced
them of their error. During the plenitude of his glory, Delfina
Guardiola, the belle of Angostura, became enraged by his
inconstancy and slammed the doors of her house in his face.
"You're a great man, General, greater than anyone," she told him.
"But love is still too big for you." He climbed through the kitchen
window and spent three days with her, and he almost lost a battle as
well as his life while he was persuading Delfina to trust in his heart.
(García Márquez 1990: 217)[16]

Manuela Saenz, his last and most interesting lover, also experiences the
general's inconstancy in personal love. Instead of leaving him or
upbraiding him about it, she remains with him. She understands his
wider vision of solidarity and love and shares his commitment to it.
Indeed, in some respects, the love that Bolívar expresses in his dream
for Latin America is the image of that of Florentino Ariza and Fermina
Daza as they take their final journey of love *up* the Magdalena River: it
is mature and all-encompassing.[17]

There is a problem with the love expressed in the vision and actions
of Bolívar though. Unlike Florentino and Fermina, Bolívar attempts to
make his vision of universal solidarity manifest by imposing it through
his power. This is a move that cannot succeed, for the presence of the
"absolute" in Bolívar's vision destroys what is most necessary for
love—the "other." Bolívar's reliance on power to achieve his vision
ends up doing to him just what power did to the visionless patriarch of
The Autumn of the Patriarch. Clearly, the vision of a great "end" for
society is no protection from damnation when the means of absolute
power are employed to achieve it. The patriarch dies an empty shell of a
man, solitary and drowned; Bolívar also drowns, but he is not an empty
shell and his solitude is mitigated by the presence of "a few friends" and
a great vision of what life and love could be.

Bolivar's vision fails because it is an attempt to impose love by
force. Political modernization cannot be forced because the use of force
denies the necessary precondition for political modernization: the real
equality of the "other."

POLITICS

It is clear that none of the three authors examined in this study believes that any vision of a better life for mankind, including that of political modernization embodied in real democracy, can be imposed on the world without nullifying its own effectiveness. The Enlightenment's political ideals of equality and democracy cannot be restored to their proper place in society by force of arms. There may be another route, though. It is less dramatic and far less certain of success, but it is an alternative that can avoid the pitfalls of absolutism. Octavio Paz calls it "criticism," and he sees it being carried out by "independent intellectuals" (Paz 1985a: 126).

For Paz, criticism is what makes a society vital. It is what gives a society the ability to change, the flexibility to be able to adapt to new circumstances and overcome problems. Criticism is the "politics" of enlightened modernity. Understood in this way, Paz says criticism has two sources: first, meaningful dialogue such as is found in independent democracies; and second, a grasp of the unique cultural truths that make up a country's individual character. (Paz often refers to the second of these as a "return to origins.")

Meaningful dialogue allows adversaries to seek peace in spite of their differences and does not fall victim to the problem of power and absolutism:

> Monologue denies the existence of the other; dialogue allows differences to remain yet at the same time creates an area in which the voices of otherness coexist and interweave. Since dialogue excludes the ultimate, it is a denial of absolutes and their despotic pretensions to totality: we are relative, and what we say and hear is relative. But this relativism is not a surrender: in order for there to be dialogue, we must affirm what we are and at the same time recognize the other in all his irreducible difference. Dialogue keeps us from denying ourselves and from denying the humanity of our adversary. (Paz 1985a: 213)

Paz sees the concept of dialogue—which he calls "one of the forms, perhaps the highest, of cosmic sympathy" (Paz 1985a: 213)—as being embodied in the idea of democracy. He even goes so far as to equate the two: "Democracy is dialogue, and dialogue paves the way for peace" (Paz 1985a: 212). Furthermore, he explains that the only way to bring about legitimate change in a country is through the dialogue of democracy. "Without democracy, changes are counterproductive; or, rather, they are not changes at all" (Paz 1985a: 188). Power, even in the service of the highest ideals, cannot effect legitimate change.

But Paz is careful to note that democracy is only an arduous process and not a miracle cure:

> Democracy is not a panacea: it is a form of living together with others, a system so that people will not kill each other, so that governments might renew themselves peacefully and presidents enter the national palace by the ballot box ["door of the vote"]. We teach ourselves democracy to live together with others and nothing more. (Paz 1990a: 131; my translation) [18]

Neither democracy nor dialogue will solve the problems of modernity, but they will help people to avoid the kinds of deadly conflicts so often provoked by absolutist ideologies. Thus the first task of the critical intellectual must be to promote dialogue (and democracy) between opposing groups.

Paz notes a second source of inspiration that the intellectual critic must grasp in order to criticize effectively. He characterizes it as a kind of deep appreciation of the unique cultural and historical traits that make up a country's character. Criticism should be rooted in the reality of a country's past. It should be progressive, but it must move forward in a way that is consistent with its own deep-seated cultural truths.

Although Paz does not specify exactly how this should happen, he gives an example. He claims that the rebellion of Emiliano Zapata, a hero of the Mexican revolution, embodied the kind of "return to origins" that is necessary to make criticism well informed:

> The Zapatistas did not conceive of Mexico as a future to be realized but as a return to origins.   The radicalism of the Mexican Revolution consisted in its originality, that is, in its return to our roots, the only proper bases for our institutions. [19]   (Paz 1985: 144) [20]

Criticism that is informed by an appreciation for these kinds of basic truths can be both traditional and radically subversive at the same time, according to Paz.

> The paradox of Zapatism lies in that it was a deeply traditionalist movement; and precisely in this traditionalism resides its

revolutionary power.   Better still: because of its traditionalism
Zapatism was radically subversive. (Paz 1985: 339) [21]

Paz is not advocating any return to subsistence farming. Instead, he
is once again painting a picture of the "absolute present" of "original
time" and embodying it in the spontaneous revolts of the Mexican
people.   Intellectual critics must be informed by these spontaneous
expressions of "the golden age" in order to remain free of absolutist
ideologies and clear about the more important concerns of everyday
people and everyday life.

> Zapata's traditionalism reveals that he had a profound
> awareness of our history. He was isolated both racially and
> regionally from the journalists and theorists of the epoch, and
> this isolation gave him the strength and insight to grasp the
> simple truth.   And the truth of the Revolution was actually
> very simple: it was the freeing of Mexican reality from the
> constricting schemes of liberalism and the abuses of the
> conservatives and neo-conservatives. (Paz 1985: 144) [22]

Criticism, Paz is saying, must avoid the pitfalls of ideologies of
either the right or the left and focus on what the people need and want
from their lives. Thus when Paz calls for a "return to origins" he is not
saying critics should offer any kind of blueprint for making society into
a mirror of a mythical past, but rather that they should keep themselves
informed about what is really most important to people right now. The
"golden age" to which Paz says all people want to return, is an image not
of any physical or temporal reality but rather an expression of the hopes
and dreams of the present generation, a "return" to the origins of the
now:

> The Zapatista movement was a return to our most ancient and
> permanent tradition...   The Revolution became an attempt to
> integrate our present and our past, or—as Leopoldo Zea put it—to
> "assimilate our history," *to change it into a living thing: a past
> made present*. This effort at integration, this return to sources,
> contrasts with the attitude of the intellectuals of the time, who not
> only failed to understand the meaning of the revolutionary
> movement but even went on playing with ideas that had no function
> whatsoever except as masks. (Paz 1985: 144; my emphasis) [23]

The political forms of liberalism and conservatism—or any other "ism," Paz implies—mask the true wants and needs of people by substituting rational systems for felt needs. The dynamic edge of Paz's call for criticism is to provide a way to move into the future without denying the "past" represented in the "return to origins," to make "our history... into a living thing" shaped by both the needs of the people and the demands of the day.

Furthermore, Paz's call for criticism to be deeply rooted in a people's cultural identity is not exclusive to the Mexican context. He sees all peoples and cultures as continually moving between the poles of identity and separation.

> It is not hard to heed that this same rhythm rules the histories of other people. I think I am dealing with a universal phenomenon. Our history is but one version of this perpetual separation and union with themselves that has been and is, life for everybody in all societies. (Paz 1999: 29)

Criticism that combines this strong sense of cultural identity with the commitment to dialogue and democracy is Paz's prescription for problems of modernity. His call for independent intellectuals to engage in a critical evaluation of the problems of modern life is an attempt to revitalize societies caught in the mire of modern rational systems. By championing ideals other than those of formal rationality, Paz hopes to awaken a new flexibility in modern states; an ability to adapt that can incorporate both the needs of rational modernity and people's need to "return" to their sources of meaning.

Of course, Paz's "criticism" is not a hard and fast solution to the problem of modernity, but perhaps that is its most compelling argument. The Enlightenment ideals of equality and democracy would be strengthened by such criticism, and the contagion of absolutist ideologies would perhaps become more containable. More importantly though, Paz's solution to the problem of modernity puts the demands of the time squarely on the shoulders of individual people living now. In this sense it matches José Ortega y Gasset's image of the social problems of all times and places. Life is, in itself and forever, shipwreck; all people can hope for in this condition is to keep afloat and do their best to rise above the abyss of the time.

Mario Vargas Llosa and Gabriel García Márquez are living examples of the kind of independent critics Paz wants to put front and center on the modern stage. Vargas Llosa, in particular, has become a vehement social critic and outspoken proponent of democracy since running for the presidency of Peru in 1990. García Márquez is a little harder to pin down (he is a personal friend of Fidel Castro and decidedly more leftist than either Paz or Vargas Llosa), but he too has been a strong advocate for the rights of Latin Americans.

Mario Vargas Llosa has been criticized for painting too negative and hopeless a picture of modern society in his novels, but even though...

> Vargas Llosa's... novels are full of frustration, pessimism, and resignation [and] their characters' futures are determined by a fall of the cards[,] the Peruvian writer does give credence to man's capacity to shuffle those cards and to continue to live within an otherwise hopeless situation. In this respect, Vargas Llosa is counting on literature to influence society. (Gerdes: 67)

Indeed, Vargas Llosa has shown that he believes the role of the intellectual in Latin American society to be much the same as the one Paz envisioned. His criticism of the mistakes of previous generations of intellectuals in Latin America came out clearly in some comments he made after publishing *The War of the End of the World*:

> You can see how intellectuals were directly responsible for a social tragedy. In the case of Canudos the Brazilian intellectuals created this ghost, this idea of a conspiracy against the Republic, this idea that Great Britain was conspiring against the Republic... Ideology placed a mist between reality and the intellectuals. People followed these ideas and they became a reality. They totally believed in the idea of a conspiracy and that was the reason for their national mobilization against the rebels. Da Cunha was one of these intellectuals. he wrote incredible articles against Canudos, telling stories about supposed English smugglers and other crazy things—in order to explain things the intellectuals couldn't explain because they didn't fit their idea of Brazil. I was fascinated with all this because this kind of process has been going on all along in Latin America. (Williams 1987: 205)

The intellectuals of Da Cunha's time made the mistake of letting themselves become blinded by ideology, yet in his fiction Vargas Llosa consistently champions the intellectuals who do not allow themselves to be swept away by any such overbearing and misleading world view. As Efraín Kristal notes, "there is indeed an important ethical dimension to Vargas Llosa's novels because his greatest literary characters, from a moral point of view, are those who make extraordinary personal sacrifices to avoid contributing to corruption and injustice" (Kristal: 198).

In his own life, Vargas Llosa has earned a reputation as one of Latin America's most unabashed social critics. His targets have included all kinds of ideological overindulgence. At a 1990 conference in Mexico City convened by Octavio Paz, for example, Vargas Llosa raised a furor by calling Mexico "the perfect dictatorship."

> The perfect dictatorship... is the dictatorship camouflaged so that it appears not to be a dictatorship. Yet, it has the characteristic of dictatorship: the permanent rule of one party. Though the Mexican system concedes sufficient space for criticism, since that criticism confirms its democratic character, it uses all methods against any criticism that endangers its permanence. (Vargas Llosa 1991: 23-24)

Against Alberto Fujimori (who beat Vargas Llosa in Peru's 1990 presidential election) Vargas Llosa's criticism is unrelenting. Despite the fact that Fujimori in fact adopted many of the free market reforms that Vargas Llosa introduced to Peruvian politics in his 1990 campaign, reforms that some critics credited for reducing Peru's hyperinflation of 8,000 percent in 1990 to 9 percent in 1995 and stimulating significant positive growth in gross domestic product figures, Vargas Llosa remains unimpressed. His reasons for being so are valid despite Fujimori's accomplishments, because when seen through the eyes of the independent critic, Fujimori's actions are revealed to be more like those of García Márquez's patriarch than the legitimate actions of a free democracy:

> Fujimori is not cleaning up corruption; he is giving it a new lease on life. And Peru has returned to the worst of times in Latin America in terms of human rights abuses. The army has a free hand to kill and torture whomever they summarily and arbitrarily choose...
> What is happening now in Peru is a classic case where practically everything... is controlled by the state...

But this kind of nostalgic order is destined to collapse and will, I fear, bring down with it the modern idea of the free-market economy. (Vargas Llosa 1993b: 55)

Though some have accused Vargas Llosa of going too far (many of whom have self-serving interests of their own to protect), it is clear that Mario Vargas Llosa is already living the life of one of Paz's independent intellectuals. He is disappointing free marketeers who were not perceptive enough to sense the ethical nature of his political stand in favor of the free market.[24]

Social inequality remains so enormous that it threatens to frustrate the process of modernization.
   The only way to avert this outcome is to make sure that the market becomes rooted in the practical life of most people. Only grass-roots modernization will do the trick. Otherwise everything is reversible because economically disenfranchised people just will not believe in the market as the instrument of progress. (Vargas Llosa 1993b: 54)

The truth is that Mario Vargas Llosa, the independent intellectual and social critic, does not see himself as belonging to any single ideology or world view. As early as 1967, when he received the Rómulo Gallegos literary prize, Vargas Llosa informed the world that the writer is the "eternal killjoy... [who goes] into battle knowing from the outset that he [will] be defeated."

It is important to remind our societies what to expect. Warn them that literature is fire, that it means nonconformity and rebellion, that the *raison d'être* of a writer is protest, disagreement and criticism... [T]he writer has been, is, and continues to be, dissatisfied... The literary vocation is born out of the disagreement between a man and the world, out of his intuition of the deficiencies, disparities and misery that surround him. Literature is a form of permanent insurrection and cannot accept strait-jackets. Any attempt to bend its angry, rebellious nature is doomed to failure. Literature might die but it will never be conformist.
   Literature can be useful to society only if it fulfills this condition. It contributes to human improvement, preventing spiritual atrophy, self-satisfaction, stagnation, human paralysis and intellectual or moral decline. Its mission is to arouse, to disturb, to alarm, to keep men in a constant state of dissatisfaction with

themselves: its function is to stimulate, without respite, the desire for change and improvement even when it is necessary to use the sharpest weapons to accomplish this task. It is essential that everyone understands this once and for all: the more critical the writings of an author against his country, the more intense will be the passion that binds him to that country. Because in the realms of literature, violence is a proof of love. (Vargas Llosa "Literature is Fire," quoted in Vargas Llosa 1996a: 71-72)

Vargas Llosa's understanding of his role has not changed with time. In 1989 he made his position as a critic independent of all ideologies even more explicit: "By itself, literature is a terrible indictment against existence under whatever regime or ideology: a blazing testimony of its insufficiencies, its inability to satisfy us. And, for this reason, it is a permanent corroder of all power structures that would like to see men satisfied and contented" (Vargas Llosa 1996a: 330). The words could have come directly from Paz's independent intellectual. In another sense, Vargas Llosa's position is evocative of José Ortega y Gasset's poor spent swimmer struggling—through the affirmation of human culture and dignity—to stay above the waves.

To play with lies, as the author and reader of fiction do, the lies that they themselves fabricate under the rule of their personal demons, is a way of affirming individual sovereignty and defending it when it is threatened; of preserving one's own free space, a citadel outside the control of power and of the interference of others, where we are truly in charge of our destiny. (Vargas Llosa 1996a: 330)

Gabriel García Márquez has not been as openly political in his public life as Vargas Llosa has, but his views are clearly expressed within his novels. He is explicit about his political stand in *One Hundred Years of Solitude*:

With *One Hundred Years*, I did want to give the idea that Latin-American history had such an oppressive reality that it had to be changed—at all costs, at any price! In any case, *One Hundred Years of Solitude* doesn't say that progress isn't possible. It says that Latin-American society is so full of frustrations and injustices that it would dishearten anyone. That really indicates a society that must be changed. (Playboy: 174)

Furthermore, García Márquez has no illusions about the role of politics
in the work of an author of fiction.

> *Todo el drama de las bananeras está planteado en mi novela de
> acuerdo con mis convicciones. El partido que yo tomo es
> definitivamente en favor de los obreros. Eso se ve claramente.
> Entonces yo creo que la gran contribución política del escritor es
> no evadirse ni de sus convicciones ni de la realidad, sino ayudar a
> que a través de su obra, el lector entienda mejor cuál es la
> realidad política y social de su país o de su continente, de su
> sociedad y creo que esa es una labor política positiva e importante
> y creo que ésa es la función política del escritor.* (García Márquez
> and Vargas Llosa: 43)

> All the drama of the banana workers is planned in my novel to
> accord with my convictions. The position that I take is definitely in
> favor of the workers. This you see clearly yourself. Then I think
> that the great political contribution of the writer is not to evade
> either his convictions or reality, but to assist them through his work,
> the reader understands best what is the political and social reality of
> his country or of his continent, of his society and I think that this is
> a positive and important political labor and I think that this is the
> political function of the writer. [my translation]

The convergence of convictions and reality has also defined García
Márquez's journalistic works. As Gloria Jeanne Bodtorf Clark (1999)
reminds us, García Márquez was first of all a journalist; he learned early
on that the techniques of journalism and fiction can be combined to
enhance the impact of both genres. "The author of a documentary
narrative has the freedom to enrich... experience as much as possible
without violating its *intencionalidad primordial*, which is to tell the
truth" (Bodtorf Clark: 101). García Márquez himself admits that
journalism is "easier than fiction": "You don't need to invent so many
elements yourself... It makes fewer stylistic and creative demands.
Conversely, you can use all the resources of fiction" (García Márquez
quoted in Bodtorf Clark: 101). In *The Story of a Shipwrecked Sailor*
(1986 [1955]), García Márquez combines his skills at writing fiction
with his convictions and the facts to tell the story of a sailor who was
washed off the deck of a Colombian destroyer in 1955. The incident
was originally censored by the Colombian government to hide the fact
that government property (the destroyer) was being used illegally to
smuggle personal property (a large volume of household appliances)

from the United States to members of the Colombian regime. García Márquez used his novelist's skills to help the sailor tell his story in a dramatic way and let other people know why seven of his fellow sailors drowned.

> *The Story of a Shipwrecked Sailor* caused an immediate political reaction as it indirectly criticized an oppressive regime. Although the story of the survival of the sailor is fascinating, the immediate purpose of the narrative is to tell why the sailors were lost in the first place. Because of censorship, this story had not been told in its entirety prior to its publication in *El Espectador*. The information which the narrative provided on the negligence of the military and the and the illegal use of government property was important in convincing the citizens of Colombia that the government was not being truthful with them. Although the publication of this story caused personal ramifications for García Márquez and Luis Velasco [the shipwrecked sailor], this narrative told the truth in a time of censorship. (Bodtorf Clark: 84)

But even outside of his writing, García Márquez has raised eyebrows with his political actions. He is a personal friend of Fidel Castro and was also good friends with Omar Torrijos, dictator of Panama, until Torrijos' death in 1981. Even so, García Márquez denies accusations that he is a communist. As for his friendship with Castro, he says...

> Ours is an intellectual friendship. It may not be widely known that Fidel is a very cultured man. When we're together, we talk a great deal about literature. Fidel is a fantastic reader...
> We don't really talk about politics *that* much. Most people find it difficult to believe that my friendship with Fidel Castro is almost totally based on our mutual interest in literature. Very few of our conversations concern the fate of the world...
> Once I remember, I left him a copy of Bram Stoker's *Dracula*, which is really an absolutely fantastic book but one that intellectuals consider unworthy. Well, I took that book to Fidel one night... That night, he had many important state documents to read and consider. Well, we talked for about an hour, and then we met again the next day at noon. "Gabriel, you screwed me!" he said. "That book; I couldn't get a minute's sleep." He'd read *Dracula* from four in the morning until 11 A.M. And *this* is an aspect of his

personality that few people know, and it is because of this that the friendship has developed. (Playboy: 67,70)

Many people do have difficulty believing that García Márquez's friendship is based primarily on a shared love of literature. And it is certainly true that García Márquez favors left-leaning solutions for Latin America. But neither of these observations prevent him from being the same kind of independent intellectual critic that Paz sees as important for the future of Latin America. It is certainly possible for an independent intellectual to favor socialist solutions over capitalist ones, for example. (In this vein, it is interesting to note that both Paz and Vargas Llosa also have had to deal with repeated attempts to label them communists or Marxists when taking stands unpopular with business interests.)

Nevertheless, there is at least one good reason to believe that García Márquez's socialist ideas are less Marxist-Leninist than philosophical. He has written a non-fiction history of Cuba that, if he were to publish it, would no doubt confirm his independent status: "What I wrote is a very harsh, very *frank* book. It would be very easy for someone to quote out of context sentences that seem against Cuba. I don't want that to happen" (Playboy: 71; emphasis original). Of course, the fact that García Márquez has not published this book is significant, but the book's very existence suggests that his friendship with Fidel Castro is personal, rather than ideological, in nature.

Beyond the questions surrounding his socialist leanings, however, no one doubts García Márquez's commitment to being a strong advocate for the rights and freedoms of the people of Latin America. His Nobel lecture in 1982 eloquently defended Latin America from both East and West:

> Why think that the social justice sought by progressive Europeans for their own countries cannot also be a goal for Latin America, with different methods for dissimilar conditions? No: the immeasurable violence and pain of our history are the result of age-old inequities and untold bitterness, and not a conspiracy plotted three thousand leagues from our home. But many European leaders and thinkers have thought so, with the childishness of old-timers who have forgotten the fruitful excesses of their youth as if it were impossible to find another destiny than to live at the mercy of the two great masters of the world. (García Márquez 1988a: 90)

The acknowledged master of the independent stance of the critical intellectual (between East and West), however, has to be Octavio Paz himself. Before his death in 1998, Paz repeatedly trounced the ideological myths of both the East and the West, associating the one with Moloch, the war god (devil) of revolution, and the other with Mammon, the god (demon) of greed and capitalism (see Paz 1985a: 128-133). In his popular writings he praised the trend toward democracy in Latin America, bid "adios" to the Sandinista regime in Nicaragua while at the same time maintaining that "the Sandinistas still have a very viable future" now that the pretensions to absolutism in their party are gone (Paz 1990b: 32), and generally advocated his vision of a critical stance based on democracy and "a way of assimilating the past but not breaking with it" (Paz 1992: 6).

In addition, and perhaps even more importantly, Paz sponsored forums to give Latin American intellectuals a platform for publicizing their critical views. These views are taken seriously in Latin America, and the very existence of such high-minded political debate has breathed new life into the democratic forms of Latin governments. The presence of this kind of dialogue even suggests the beginnings of what Latin America has most lacked since its decision to become "Liberal" after the civil wars of the nineteenth century: a participatory tradition of grassroots democracy embedded within a culture of democracy and toleration.

CRITICISM AND DIGNITY IN LIFE

Modern man likes to pretend that his thinking is wide-awake. But this wide-awake thinking has led us into the mazes of a nightmare in which the torture chambers are endlessly repeated in the mirrors of reason. When we emerge, perhaps we will realize that we have been dreaming with our eyes open, and that the dreams of reason are intolerable. And then, perhaps, we will begin to dream once more with our eyes closed.[25]

> Octavio Paz (1985: 212)
> *The Labyrinth of Solitude*

Simón Bolívar once wrote: "There is no trust in the Americas, neither in individuals nor in nations: the constitutions are books, the treaties scraps of paper, the elections battles, liberty is anarchy, and life a torture" (Simón Bolívar, 1815; quoted in Como: 53). In the time since Bolívar penned these words much has changed. The "masks" of reality are slipping off of the hidden patriarchal forms and mechanisms of government in Latin America, and people are becoming aware of the possibility of achieving a new level of dignity in modern life. Through criticism of the kind advocated by Octavio Paz, Latin Americans are coming to grips with the political and cultural problems of modernity and discovering new ways to live with the horrors of the twentieth and twenty-first centuries.

> Passive indifference to values is perhaps the real evil of the liberal societies. It is, in fact, a form of nihilism. So the irony of modern life... is that the freedom to create is also the freedom that destroys. (Paz 1991: 38).

> The real menace lies in the inability of modernity to find a way to reconcile itself with the values of tradition, of a way to reconcile social and individual values. (Paz 1991: 38-39).

Paz found a way to reconcile these values in his poetic understanding of the "present moment." Through critical appreciation of the values that animate the life of a people (i.e. the "return to origins") and dialogue (i.e. "democracy"), the values of tradition can be assimilated into an ethics of the "now":

> The decline of the ideologies I have called metahistorical, by which I mean those that assign to history a goal and a direction, implies the tacit abandonment of global solutions. With good sense, we tend more and more toward limited remedies to solve concrete problems. It is prudent to abstain from legislating about the future. Yet the present requires much more than attention to immediate needs; it demands global soul-searching. For a long time I have firmly believed that the twilight of the future heralds the advent of the now. To think about the now means first of all to recover the critical vision. (Paz 1985: 30)

> What we need to build now is not only an aesthetics and poetics of the convergent moment, but an ethics and a politics that follow from this perception of time and reality.
> In such a new civilization, the present would not be sacrificed for the future or for eternity. Nor would the present be lived, as consumer societies do, in the denial of death. Rather, we would live

in the full freedom of our diversity and sensuality in the certain knowledge of death.

The ethical foundations of the new civilization would extol this freedom and creativity without illusion; it would seek to preserve the plurality of the present—the plurality of different times and the presence of the "other." Its politics would be a dialogue of cultures. (Paz 1992: 7)

Paz's vision of the "new civilization" does not deny the problems of divided modernity, nor does it wish them away with a new absolutism. It is, on the contrary, in complete harmony with the fact that life will always be fraught with problems. It is also perfectly tuned to José Ortega y Gasset's understanding of life as shipwreck. The contradictions of modern life will continue to cast a shadow over humanity in the twenty-first century, just as the problems of life have always done and certainly will continue to do long after our own time has passed into oblivion. But Paz's testimony already sounds like that of a man convinced that the future, and the "now," are full of hope for humanity. "Deliverance" is still possible. Certainly it will not be the *deus ex machina* so many look and hope for today, but there is a kind of "deliverance" in simple human dignity. There is dignity in the struggle of modern life, and so long as we continue to struggle on in spite of it all, there will be dignity and beauty in the time to come—perhaps all the more than if the struggle were not so challenging.

We have not solved these contradictions, but with them and through them we have created a truly original culture. We are alive at the end of the 20th century. (Paz 1991: 41)

---

1. *La única arma eficaz contra las ortodoxias es la crítica; para defendernos de las intolerancia y de los fanatismos no tenemos más recurso que ejercer, con firmeza pero con lucidez, dos virtudes opuestas: la tolerancia y la libertad de espíritu.* (Paz 1978: 458)
2. See Samuel Huntington, *Political Order in Changing Societies* (1968) for an intelligent presentation of this argument.
3. For the original Spanish text, see Paz, 1984, page 183.
4. For the original Spanish text, see Paz, 1984, pages 163-164.
5. For a fascinating and eloquent history of *caudillo* rule in Mexico,

see Enrique Krauze's *Mexico: Biography of Power* (HarperCollins, 1997).

6. For the original Spanish text, see Paz, 1984, page 164.

7. For the original Spanish text, see Paz, 1967, page 202.

8. *Historia de Mayta* (1984), *La guerra del fin del mundo* (1981) and Lituma en los Andes (1993).

9. The events in question actually did take place and form the basis for a classic text in Brazilian literature: *Os Sertões* (1902) by Euclides da Cunha, which has been translated into English as *Rebellion in the Backlands* (1944).

10. In his memoirs, Vargas Llosa recalls once being called "subhuman" [*subhombre*] during a meeting of student communists at San Marcos University. He describes the accusation as "devastating" [*devastadora*] (Vargas Llosa 1994: 245; 1993: 247).

11. *Death in the Andes*, pp. 8-16; *Lituma en los Andes*, pp. 17-25.

12. *Death in the Andes*, pp. 88-103; *Lituma en los Andes*, pp. 106-122.

13. In several interviews, García Márquez has pointed out that one of the greatest compliments ever given to his book came from his friend Omar Torrijos (dictator of Panama before his death in 1981), who said "We are all just as you describe" (Mendoza and García Márquez 1983: 88) ["*Todos somos así como tú dices*" (Mendoza and García Márquez 1982: 89)].

14. *El general en su laberinto* (1989).

15. See Michael Bell (1993), chapter 8, for more on this theme.

16. For the original Spanish text, see García Márquez, 1989, page 221.

17. The contrasting images of sailing up and down the river is another interesting parallel here. The vision is the same, but love succeeds where power does not.

18. *La democracia no es una panacea: es una forma de convivencia, un sistema para que la gente no se mate, para que los gobiernos se renueven pacíficamente y los presidentes entren en el Palacio presidencial por la puerta del voto. La democracia nos enseña a convivir y nada más.* (Paz 1990a:131)

19. Note that Paz is referring here to the Zapatistas of the Mexican Revolution (1910-1920), not the Zapatistas associated with the recent uprising in the Mexican state of Chiapas.

20. For the original Spanish text, see Paz, 1959, page 130.

21. For the original Spanish text, see Paz, 1975, page 235.

22. For the original Spanish text, see Paz, 1959, page 130.

23. For the original Spanish text, see Paz, 1959, page 130.

24. James Como of *National Review* is one such free marketeer. *National Review* strongly supported Vargas Llosa in his presidential bid, but now looks approvingly on Fujimori's reforms (and disapprovingly on Vargas Llosa's criticism; see Como: 72). Since Fujimori's reforms have favored foreign interests over domestic ownership, one cannot be too surprised at this self-serving hypocrisy.

25. For the original Spanish text, see Paz, 1959, page 191.

BIBLIOGRAPHY OF WORKS CITED

Acosta Cruz, María Isabel. 1989. "Writer-Speaker? Speaker-Writer? Narrative and Cultural Intervention in Mario Vargas Llosa's *El Hablador.*" *Inti* 29-30: 133-145.

Adorno, Theodor. 1983. *Aesthetic Theory.* Boston: Routledge.

Althusser, Louis. 1996. *For Marx.* Trans. Ben Brewster. New York: Verso Books.

Avineri, Shlomo. 1968. *The Social and Political Thought of Karl Marx.* Cambridge: Cambridge University Press.

Bell, Daniel. 1976. *The Cultural Contradictions of Capitalism.* New York: Basic Books.

Bell, Michael. 1993. *Gabriel García Márquez: Solitude and Solidarity.* London: MacMillan.

Berger, Peter L. 1975. *Pyramids of Sacrifice: Political Ethos and Social Change.* New York: Basic Books.

Berman, Marshall. 1988. *All That Is Solid Melts Into Air: The Experience of Modernity.* New York: Penguin Books.

Bloom, Alan. 1987. *The Closing of the American Mind: How Higher Education has Failed Democracy and Impoverished the Souls of Today's Students.* New York: Simon and Schuster.

Bloom, Harold. 1989. *Modern Critical Views: Gabriel García Márquez.* Ed. Harold Bloom. New York: Chelsea House Publishers.

Bodtorf Clark, Gloria Jeanne. 1999. *A Synergy of Styles: Art and Artifact in Gabriel García Márquez.* New York: University Press of America.

Cantor, Jay. 1981. *The Space Between: Literature and Politics.* Baltimore: The Johns Hopkins University Press.

Castro-Klarén, Sara. 1990. *Understanding Mario Vargas Llosa.* Columbia, SC: University of South Carolina Press.

Cheuse, Alan. 1977. "Mario Vargas Llosa and Conversation in the Cathedral: The Question of Naturalism." *Texas Studies in Literature and Language* XIX, 4 (winter): 445-451.

Christ, Ronald. 1978. "Talk with Vargas Llosa." *The New York Times Book Review*, 9 April 1978, p. 33.

_____. 1975. "Novel Form, Novel Sense." *Review* 14: 30-36.

Christie, John S. 1993. "Fathers and Virgins: García Márquez's Faulknerian *Chronicle of a Death Foretold*." *Latin American Literary Review* XXI, 41 (Jan-June): 21-29)

Como, James. 1995. "Hero Storyteller." *National Review* (April 17): 53-56, 72.

Crawford, W. R. A. 1963. *A Century of Latin American Political Thought.* Cambridge: Harvard University Press.

Da Cunha, Euclydes. 1944. *Rebellion in the Backlands.* Trans. Samuel Putnam. Chicago: University of Chicago Press.

_____. 1902. *Os Sertões.* Rio de Janeiro: Livraria Francisco Alves.

Davis, Harold Eugene. 1972. *Latin American Thought: A Historical Introduction.* New York: Free Press.

_____. 1961. *Latin American Social Thought.* Washington D.C.: University Press of Washington.

Davis, Mary. 1978. "Mario Vargas Llosa: The Necessary Scapegoat." *Texas Studies in Literature and Language* XIX, 4 (winter): 530-543.

Diez, Luys A. 1978. "The Sources of *The Green House*: The Mythical Background of a Fabulous Novel." In *Mario Vargas Llosa: A Collection of Critical Essays.* Ed. Charles Rossman and Alan Warren Friedman. Austin: University of Texas Press.

Dobson, Andrew. 1989. *An Introduction to the Politics and Philosophy of José Ortega y Gasset.* New York: Cambridge University Press.

Durkheim, Emile. 1915. *The Elementary Forms of the Religious Life.* Trans. Joseph Ward Swain. New York: Free Press.

Dust, Patrick H. 1989. "Freedom, Power and Culture in Ortega y Gasset's Philosophy of Technology." In *Ortega y Gasset and the Question of Modernity*, ed. by Patrick H. Dust. Minneapolis, MN: The Prisma Institute.

Edelman, Murray. 1988. *Constructing the Political Spectacle.* Chicago: University of Chicago Press.

_____. 1967. *The Symbolic Uses of Politics*. Chicago: Unviersity of Illinois Press.

Edwards, Jorge. 1975. "The Serpent of Remorse." Trans. Tom J. Lewis. *Review* 14: 22-25.

Fernández de Lizardi, José Joaquín. 1942. *The Itching Parrot*. Trans. Eugene Pressly & Katherine Anne Porter. New York: Doubleday.

_____. 1824. *Conversaciones del payo y el sacristán*. Translated excerpts in Harold E. Davis, *Latin American Social Thought*, 1961: 39-55.

Feustle, Joseph A. 1978. "Mario Vargas Llosa: A Labyrinth of Solitude." In *Mario Vargas Llosa: A Collection of Critical Essays*. Ed. Charles Rossman and Alan Warren Friedman. Austin: University of Texas Press.

Foster, David William. 1969. "García Márquez and Solitude." *Américas* 21, 11-12 (Nov-Dec): 36-41.

Foucault, Michel. 1978. *The History of Sexuality* New York: Pantheon Books.

Freud, Sigmund. 1961. *Civilization and Its Discontents*. Ed. & Trans. James Strachey. New York: W. W. Norton & Co.

García Márquez, Gabriel. 1990. *The General in His Labyrinth*. Trans. Edith Grossman. New York: Penguin Books.

_____. 1989. *El general en su laberinto*. Buenos Aires: Editorial Sudamericana.

_____. 1988 [1982]. "The Solitude of Latin America (Nobel Lecture, 1982)." Trans. Marina Castañeda. In *Gabriel García Márquez and the Powers of Fiction*. Ed. Julio Ortega. Austin: University of Texas Press.

_____. 1988a. *Love in the Time of Cholera*. Trans. Edith Grossman. New York: Penguin Books.

_____. 1986. *The Story of a Shipwrecked Sailor*. Trans. Randolph Hogan. New York: Vintage Books.

_____. 1985. *El amor en los tiempos del colera*. Bogotá: La Oveja Negra.

_____. 1983. *Chronicle of a Death Foretold*. Trans. Gregory Rabassa. New York: Alfred A Knopf.

_____. 1981. *Crónica de una muerte anunciada*. Bogotá: La Oveja Negra.

_____. 1976. *The Autumn of the Patriarch*. Trans. Gregory Rabassa. New York: Avon Books.

_____. 1975. *El otoño del patriarca*. Barcelona: Plaza & Janes.

_____. 1972. *Leaf Storm and Other Stories by Gabriel García Márquez.* Trans. Gregory Rabassa. New York: Harper and Row.

_____. 1970. *One Hundred Years of Solitude.* Trans. Gregory Rabassa. New York: Harper.

_____. 1968. *No One Writes to the Colonel and Other Stories by Gabriel García Márquez.* Trans. J. S. Bernstein. New York: Harper and Row.

_____. 1967. *Cien años de soledad.* Buenos Aires: Sudamericana.

García Márquez, Gabriel and Mario Vargas Llosa. 1967. *La novela en America Latina: dialogo.* Lima: Universidad nacional de Ingenieria.

Gerdes, Dick. 1985. *Mario Vargas Llosa.* Boston: Twayne Publishers.

Gramsci, Antonio. 1985. *Selections from Cultural Writings.* Ed. David Forgacs and Geoffrey Nowell-Smith. Trans. William Boelhower. London: Lawrence and Wishart.

Grey, Rockwell. 1989. *The Imperative of Modernity: An Intellectual Biography of José Ortega y Gasset.* Berkeley: University of California Press.

Hancock, Joel. 1975. "Animalization and Chiaroscuro Techniques: Descriptive Language in *La ciudad y los perros* (The City and the Dogs)." *Latin American Literary Review* 4(7): 37-47.

Hennis, Wilhelm. 1987. *Max Weber: Essays in Reconstruction.* Translated by Keith Tribe. Boston: Allen & Unwin.

Holston, James. 1989. *The Modernist City: An Anthropological Critique of Brasília.* Chicago: University of Chicago Press.

Horkheimer, Max and Theodor Adorno. 1972. *The Dialectic of Enlightenment.* Trans. John Comming. New York: Herder and Herder.

Huntington, Samuel. 1968. *Political Order in Changing Societies.* New Haven: Yale University Press.

ICA Video. 1984. "Mario Vargas Llosa with John King." [Videorecording] London: Institute of Contemporary Arts.

Kerr, Clark. 1991. "Ortega y Gasset for the 21st Century: Mission of the University Reexamined." *Society,* September/October.

Kovács, Katherine S. 1984. "The Bureaucratization of Knowledge and Sex in Flaubert and Vargas Llosa." *Comparative Literature Studies* 21(1): 30-51.

Kristal, Efraín. 1998. *Temptation of the Word: The Novels of Mario Vargas Llosa.* Nashville: Vanderbilt University Press.

Levitt, Morton P. 1986. "From Realism to Magic Realism: The Meticulous Modernist Fictions of García Márquez." In *Critical*

Perspectives on Gabriel García Márquez. Ed. Bradley A. Shaw and Nora Vera-Godwin. Lincoln, Nebraska: Society of Spanish and Spanish-American Studies.

Lipski, John M. 1979. "Narrative Textures in *Conversation in the Cathedral*." *Revista de Estudios Hispánicos* 13: 66-79.

Lyotard, Jean-Francois. 1984. *The Postmodern Condition: A Report on Knowledge*. Trans. Geoff Bennington and Brian Massumi. Minneapolis: Univeristy of Minnesota Press.

Marcuse, Herbert. 1964. *One-Dimensional Man*. Boston: Beacon Press.

Martin, Gerald. 1987. "On <magical' and social realism in García Márquez." In *Gabriel García Márquez: New Readings*. Ed. Bernard McGuirk and Richard Cardwell. New York: Cambridge University Press.

McGuirk, Bernard and Richard Cardwell. 1987. *Gabriel García Márquez: New Readings*. New York: Cambridge University Press.

McInnes, Neil. 1967. "Ortega y Gasset, José." Vol. 6 of *The Encyclopedia of Philosophy*. New York: The Macmillan Company and the Free Press.

McMurray, George R., Ed. 1987. *Critical Essays on Gabriel García Márquez*. Ed. George R. McMurray. Boston: G. K. Hall & Co.

_____. 1977. *Gabriel García Márquez*. New York: Frederick Ungar Publishing Co.

McNerney, Kathleen. 1989. *Understanding Gabriel García Márquez*. Columbia, S.C.: University of South Carolina Press.

Mendoza, Plinio Apuleyo and Gabriel García Márquez. 1983. *The Fragrance of Guava*. Trans. Ann Wright. Norfolk, V.A.: The Thetford Press Ltd.

Mendoza, Plinio Apuleyo and Gabriel García Márquez. 1982. *El olor de la guayaba*. Barcelona: Bruguera.

Merrel, Floyd. 1973. "Jose Arcadio Buendía's Scientific Paradigms: Man in Search of Himself." *Latin American Literary Review* II, 3 (Fall-Winter): 59-70.

Moody, Michael. 1977. "A Small Whirlpool: Narrative Structure in *The Green House*." *Texas Studies in Literature and Language* XIX, 4 (winter): 408-427.

Moreno Turner, Fernando. 1975. "A Complex Space." Trans. Renata M. Treitel. *Review* 14: 26-29.

Nietzsche, Friedrich. 1969. *On the Genealogy of Morals and Ecce Homo*. Ed. & Trans. Walter Kaufman. New York: Vintage Books.

_____. 1967. *Thus Spake Zarathustra*. Ed. & Trans. Walter Kaufman. New York: Heritage Press.

Ortega y Gasset, Jose. 1961. *The Modern Theme*. Trans. James Cleugh. New York: Harper.

_____. 1957. *Man and People*. Trans. W. Trask. New York: W. W. Norton & Co.

_____. 1956. "In Search of Goethe from Within." *The Dehumanization of Art and Other Writings on Art and Culture*. Trans. Williard Trask. New York: Doubleday Anchor.

_____. 1932. *The Revolt of the Masses*. Trans. Anonymous. New York: W. W. Norton & Co.

Ortega, Julio. 1988. *Gabriel García Márquez and the Powers of Fiction*. Ed. Julio Ortega. Austin: University of Texas Press.

Paz, Octavio. 1999. *Itinerary*. Trans. Jason Wilson. London: Menard Press.

_____. 1992. "West Turns East at the End of History." *New Perspectives Quarterly* (Spring): 5-9.

_____. 1991. "Contiguous Geography, Homogeneous Reality?" *New Perspectives Quarterly* (Winter): 36-41.

_____. 1990. *Octavio Paz: In Search of the Present, 1990 Nobel Lecture*. Bilingual Edition. New York: Harcourt Brace Jovanovich.

_____. 1990a. *Pequeña crónica de grandes días*. Mexico City: Fondo de Cultura Economica.

_____. 1990b. "Adios, Sandinistas." *New Perspectives Quarterly* (Spring): 32-33.

_____. 1987. *The Collected Poems of Octavio Paz: 1957-1987*. Ed. & Trans. Eliot Weinberger. New York: New Directions.

_____. 1985. *The Labyrinth of Solitude and The Other Mexico, Return to the Labyrinth of Solitude, Mexico and the United States, the Philanthropic Ogre*. Trans. Lysander Kemp, Yara Milos, and Rachel Phillips Belash. New York: Grove Press Inc.

_____. 1985a. *One Earth, Four or Five Worlds: Reflections on Contemporary History*. Trans. Helen R. Lane. New York: Harcourt Brace Jovanovich.

_____. 1984. *Tiempo nublado*. Barcelona: Seix Barral.

_____. 1983. *Alternating Current*. Trans. Helen Lane. New York: Little, Brown and Company.

_____. 1978. "*México y Estados Unidos: posiciones y contraposiciones*" in *México en la obra de Octavio Paz*. Ed. Octavio

Paz and Luis Mario Schneider. Mexico City: Fondo de Cultura Económica, 1987: 436-459.

_____. 1975. "*Vuelta a "El laberinto de la soledad" (Conversación con Claude Fell)*" in *México en la obra de Octavio Paz*. Ed. Octavio Paz and Luis Mario Schneider. Mexico City: Fondo de Cultura Económica, 1987: 224-251.

_____. 1974. *Conjunctions and Disjunctions*. Trans. Helen Lane. New York: Viking Press.

_____. 1967. *Corriente Alterna*. Mexico City: *Siglo XXI Editores, S. A.*

_____. 1959. *El laberinto de la soledad*. Mexico City: Fondo de Cultura Económica.

_____. 1950. "*Todos santos, día de muertos*" in *México en la obra de Octavio Paz*. Ed. Octavio Paz and Luis Mario Schneider. Mexico City: Fondo de Cultura Económica, 1987: 35-54.

_____. 1950a. "*Los hijos de la malinche*" in *México en la obra de Octavio Paz*. Ed. Octavio Paz and Luis Mario Schneider. Mexico City: Fondo de Cultura Económica, 1987: 55-79.

Paz, Octavio and Luis Mario Schneider, eds. 1987a. *México en la obra de Octavio Paz: Volume I, El peregrino en su patria*. Mexico City: Fondo de Cultura Económica.

"Playboy Interview: Gabriel García Márquez." 1983.*Playboy*, 30,2 (February): 65-67, 70-77, 172-178.

Pellicani, Luciano. 1986-87. "Ortega's Theory of Social Action."*Telos*. 70:115-124.

Pope, Randolph D. 1987. "Transparency and Illusion in García Márquez's *Chronicle of a Death Foretold*." *Latin American Literary Review* 15 (January-June): 183-200.

Quiroga, José. 1999. *Understanding Octavio Paz*. Columbia: University of South Carolina Press.

Rabassa, Gregory. 1975. "A Conversation with the Translator."*Review* 14: 17-21.

Rodo, Jose Enrique. 1988. *Ariel*. Austin: University of Texas Press.

Rodríguez Monegal, Emir. 1987. "*One Hundred Years of Solitude*: The Last Three Pages." In *Critical Essays on Gabriel García Márquez*. Ed. George R. McMurray. Boston: G. K. Hall & Co.

Rorty, Richard. 1985. "Habermas and Lyotard on Postmodernty." In *Habermas and Modernity*, pp. 161-175. Edited by Richard J. Bernstein. Cambridge: The MIT Press.

_____. 1979. *Philosophy and the Mirror of Nature*. Princeton: Princeton University Press.

Rossman, Charles and Alan Warren Friedman, eds. 1978. *Mario Vargas Llosa: A Collection of Critical Essays*. Austin: University of Texas Press.

Sarmiento, Domingo Faustino. 1972. *Facundo: Life in the Argentine Republic in the Days of the Tyrants, or, Civilization and Barbarism*. Trans. H. Mann. New York: Hafner Press.

Scaff, Lawrence A. 1989. *Fleeing the Iron Cage: Culture, Politics, and Modernity in the Thought of Max Weber*. Berkeley: University of California Press.

Selznick, Philip. 1992. *The Moral Commonwealth: Social Theory and the Promise of Community*. Berkeley: University of California Press.

Shaffer, Peter. 1973. *Equus: A Play in Two Acts*. New York: Samuel French, Inc.

Shakespeare, William. 1960. *Julius Caesar*. New York: Penguin Books.

_____. 1956. *Macbeth*. New York: Penguin Books.

Shaw, Bradley A. and Nora Vera-Godwin, Eds. 1986. *Critical Perspectives on Gabriel García Márquez*. Lincoln, Nebraska: Society of Spanish and Spanish-American Studies.

Simmel, Georg. 1978. *The Philosophy of Money*. Translated by Tom Bottomore and David Frisby. Boston: Routledge and Kegan Paul.

Sims, Robert Lewis. 1981. *The Evolution of Myth in García Márquez from La Hojarsca to Cien Años de Soledad*. Miami: Ediciones Universal.

Sinclair, Upton. 1951. *The Jungle*. New York: Harper.

Tillich, Paul. 1957. *Dynamics of Faith*. New York: Harper & Row.

Vargas Llosa, Mario. 1996. *Death in the Andes*. Trans. Edith Grossman. New York: Penguin Books.

_____. 1996a. *Making Waves*. Trans. John King. New York: Penguin Books.

_____. 1993. *Lituma en los Andes*. Barcelona: Planeta.

_____. 1994. *A Fish in the Water: A Memoir*. Trans. Helen Lane. New York: Farrar, Straus and Giroux.

_____. 1993. *El pez en el agua: Memorias*. Barcelona: Seix Barral.

_____. 1993. "Torture Without Inflation." *New Perspectives Quarterly* (Fall): 53-55.

_____. 1991. "Mexico: The Perfect Dictator-ship." *New Perspectives Quarterly* (Winter): 23-24.

_____. 1989 [1971]. "García Márquez: From Aracataca to Macondo." In *Modern Critical Views: Gabriel García Márquez*. Ed. Harold Bloom. New York: Chelsea House Publishers.

_____. 1989a. *The Storyteller.* Trans. Helen Lane. New York: Farrar, Straus and Giroux.

_____. 1987. *El hablador.* Barcelona: Seix Barral.

_____. 1986. *The Real Life of Alejandro Mayta.* Trans. Alfred Mac Adam. New York: Farrar, Straus, and Giroux.

_____. 1986a. *The Perpetual Orgy: Flaubert & Madame Bovary.* Trans. Helen Lane. New York: Farrar, Straus, Giroux.

_____. 1984. *Historia de Mayta.* Barcelona: Seix Barral.

_____. 1982. *The War of the End of the World.* Trans. Helen Lane. New York: Harper.

_____. 1982a. *Aunt Julia and the Scriptwriter.* Trans. Helen R. Lane. New York: Avon Books.

_____. 1981. *La guerra del fin del mundo.* Barcelona: Seix Barral.

_____. 1978. *Captain Pantoja and the Special Service.* Trans. Gregory Kolovakos & Ronald Christ. New York: Farrar, Straus, and Giroux.

_____. 1977. *La tia Julia y el escribidor.* Barcelona: Seix Barral.

_____. 1975. *Conversation in the Cathedral.* Trans. Gregory Rabassa. New York: Harper.

_____. 1975a. *La orgía perpetua.* Barcelona: Seix Barral.

_____. 1973. *Pantaleón y las visitadoras.* Barcelona: Seix Barral.

_____. 1969. *Conversación en La Catedral.* Barcelona: Seix Barral.

_____. 1968. *The Green House.* Trans. Gregory Rabassa. New York: Harper.

_____. 1966. *La casa verde.* Barcelona: Seix Barral.

_____. 1966. *The Time of the Hero.* Trans. Lysander Kemp. New York: Grove Press.

_____. 1965. *La ciudad y los perros.* Barcelona: Seix Barral.

Warren, Robert Penn. 1946. *All the King's Men.* New York: Time Inc.

Watson, Richard A. 1987. "A Pig's Tail." *Latin American Literary Review* 15 (Jan-June): 89-92.

Weber, Max. 1968. *Economy and Society.* Edited by Guenther Roth and Claus Wittich. Berkeley: University of California Press.

_____. 1958. *The Protestant Ethic and the Spirit of Capitalism.* Trans. Talcott Parsons. New York: Charles Scribner's Sons.

_____. 1946. "Science as a Vocation." In *From Max Weber: Essays in Sociology.* Translated and Edited by H. H. Gerth and C. Wright Mills. New York: Oxford University Press.

Wellmer, Albrecht. 1985. "Reason, Utopia, and the *Dialectic of Enlightenment.*" In *Habermas and Modernity.* Edited by Richard J. Bernstein. Cambridge: The MIT Press.

Williams, Raymond Leslie. 1987. "The Boom Twenty Years Later: An Interview with Mario Vargas Llosa." *Latin American Literary Review* 15 (January-June): 201-206.

_____. 1986. *Mario Vargas Llosa*. New York: Ungar.

_____. 1978. "The Narrative Art of Mario Vargas Llosa: Two Organizing Principles in *Pantaleón y las visitadoras*".In *Mario Varga Llosa: A Collection of Critical Essays*. Ed. Charles Rossman and Alan Warren Friedman. Austin: University of Texas Press.

Wilson, Jason. 1986. *Octavio Paz*. Boston: Twayne.

Wood, Michael. 1990. *Gabriel García Márquez: One Hundred Years of Solitude*. Cambridge: Cambridge University Press.

INDEX

absolute present (See time:
    absolute present)
Adorno, Theodor, 56n8, 68n2
Alienation, 13, 24, 32, 36, 107,
    109
Althusser, Louis, 68n2
Ariel (Rodó), 66
art: 57-58; aesthetics, 153; and
    politcs, 57-58, 63, 68n1
asceticism, 33-34
ascetic ideal, 25n3, 27-32
atheism, 29
Aunt Julia and the Scriptwriter
    (Vargas Llosa), 110
Autumn of the Patriarch, The
    (García Márquez), 78, 79-80,
    90, 99-100, 138, 140
Baxter, Richard, 34
Bell, Daniel, 11-13, 18, 20, 22, 24,
    33, 47-48, 50, 52, 45n6
Bell, Michael, 155n15
Berman, Marshall, 3, 68n5-7

Biely, Andrei, 64
Bloom, Alan, 2
Bolívar, Simón, 134, 138-140,
    152-153
Bodtorf Clark, Gloria Jeanne, 149
Brasilia, Brazil, 61-64, 68n6
bureaucracy, 14, 35, 106-109, 129
Cantor, Jay, 57
capitialism, 7, 32, 34-36, 43, 47,
    61, 129, 134, 136, 151-152
*Captain Pantoja and the Special
    Service* (Vargas Llosa),
    106-110
Castro, Fidel, 132, 134, 150-151
characteristic transformations of
    modernity: 6-15, 24, 26, 37;
    defined, 6; fragmentation and
    specialization, 6-8, 37,
    112-114, 125-126;
    rationalization, 14-15, 17, 20,
    23-24, 34, 37, 107-108;
    secularization, 9-10, 17, 34,